This memoir is dedicated to D. B. for selflessly giving us our miracle boy.

It is written for Viktor Zaba Yonkers who gives me hope and great joy.

ACKNOWLEDGMENTS

To Ed who has taken this entire trip with me—through the good times and the bad; to Shara—our other miracle—and to her family—especially Tyler and Trevor—my South Carolina joys who keep me focused; to Laura who keeps us blessedly close; to all "sisters and friends of my heart"—Mary Hinton, Lana and John Watson, and Rhonda Wilson; to my sorority sisters—Janie Donlon, Joyce Holobaugh, Sara Petti, Fran Weaver, Nancy Brown, Linda Parks, and Judy Saurino who was the first of us to lose a precious son.

To my Mom and Dad whose loss allowed me to know I had the strength to survive losing our only son.

And to all our relatives and friends throughout the years who knew and cared about Michael, too—you all have given me the strength to keep on keeping on.

Last, I would like to say "thank you" to Dr. Nancy Smith for suggesting I journal the good memories.

FAU

Michael's College Graduation

2000

Sorority Sisters: Joyce, Nancy, Sara   Me, Janie, Linda, Judy and Fran

Mary

Viktor and Donald

Michael and Laura

Ed, Shara, Tyler, and Trevor

John, Me and Lana in Boston

Rhonda

Covitz Wedding

Debbie and Erik's

1

No question. Michael *was* a miracle baby! He was exactly what I had promised his daddy in the fall of 1971---my promise?—that Ed would have his own baby boy. In August of 1971, I was told that I needed surgery---surgery that would take away my ability to have any children. Ed and I were going to be married on September 9th of that year, but we had to put it off until October 3rd as I needed time to recover from the surgery. Meanwhile, my gynecologist, Dr. M. Crispin, was promising us that he would help us get our family.

The following Christmas (1972) we thought we were going to begin our family---our first baby. A doctor friend of Dr. Crispin's who practiced in St. Petersburg contacted Dr. Crispin and told him that he had a baby for us. We named her Dayna Lynne---but she was not going to be coming home with us because her birth mom changed her mind and wanted to keep her. The lawyer (Allen Samuels) in St. Petersburg, who represented Dayna's family felt terrible for us and promised he would find us a baby of our own. On January 12, 1973 this lawyer---who was a stranger to us---came through on his promise! He called us and told us to come get our son!

We hurried across the state to Bay Front Medical Center in St. Petersburg---I think it was VERY early on January 15th---to pick up our baby boy. We brought with us a blue snap-in-front gown (I was petrified to think of pulling something over the baby's head—so afraid I would hurt him!) and his first pair of moccasins---just like his daddy wore. Of course those moccasins wobbled on his tiny feet. Our first look at our son was magical and amazing---he was so small--- 7lbs. 4oz. and 19 3/4 in. long--and he was a precious baldy bean. He didn't cry---just made wonderful cooing noises like he was so comfortable in his world. We quickly said our "goodbyes" to all the nurses who raved over what a good baby Michael was and went out to our car. I sat with Michael in my lap and counted all his little fingers and toes---I don't know why because he was ours---PERIOD—and it didn't matter how many he had or didn't have. But I guess this is just a natural, time-honored tradition, and all new parents do it. In fact I was to see Michael do the very same thing 35 years later when he was looking at Viktor Zaba—his very own brand new, beautiful baby boy!

Anyway, still sitting in the car and staring at our miracle baby boy, I remember feeling extreme happiness—giddy and in wonder. I told Ed that I thought we needed to hurry away from that hospital before Michael's biological family changed their minds!! We decided to stop by Mr. Samuel's office to thank him and show him what happiness he had given us. There were a ton of pictures all along his walls---like a mural---of smiling babies and their families. It was obvious that he didn't arrange adoptions for the money---he did it to make happy families; at least that was my impression after visiting his office. We said goodbye to the man who had helped make our dream come true, and we hurried back to our little apartment in Lake Park with our precious little boy—a real miracle.

Now, on our way home from the hospital—a rather lengthy 3 and ½ hour ride—I got out the formula bottle that the nurses had given to us---to feed our very hungry baby. The bottle was unlike any I had ever seen before---resembling a small doll's pretend-bottle. Michael took the little nipple quickly into his mouth and began to suck with vigor. He sucked on that bottle as we traveled across the middle of Florida on that lonely two-lane stretch of road called RT. 60. But the formula never drained at all from the bottle! I thought that he must be having trouble with his ability to suck, and after a long while, he was noticeably tired of sucking and pushed the bottle out of his little mouth. I took the bottle and looked at it closely. I couldn't believe what I found!! There was a seal still in place at the top of the bottle---he hadn't gotten any sustenance---no formula at all for his hungry tummy! But he didn't cry—not at all—and after I removed the seal from the bottle top, he took the bottle and drank thirstily. He fell asleep about half way through the bottle, exhausted from all his sucking effort! Later, he awoke crying, "change my dirty diaper" which I did post haste---feeling *very* guilty about starving my little boy.

Pay attention because the telling of the PBF saga (i.e. Plastic Bag Family) is about to begin--- the PBF explanation will have to be brought up in the telling of ensuing chapters about Michael's life. Suffice it to say that I forgot to bring the all-important plastic bag in which to place soiled diapers for safe keeping---until we could dispose of them later. Somewhere between St. Petersburg and Yeehaw Junction there is a very soiled diaper---still not decomposed after 36 years!!! I humbly ask for forgiveness from Earth and Green lovers everywhere. Despite these calamities, we made it home to Lake Park and got cozy with our baby boy.

Sometimes the present gets into my head when I am trying to write about "long ago." Like I read something or hear a joke I so want to share with Michael—the adult Michael. He is such a miracle in so many ways. He's smart and funny---definitely fun to do things with---exciting to talk to, spontaneous to play with, and trusting enough with whom to share life's mysteries.

I have always loved to teach, but teaching Michael was the most fun! (I loved to teach Shara, too, later when she came to live with us---miracle # 2.) Michael didn't talk early, but he certainly loved to listen---at least he acted like he loved it! (Viktor Zaba is the same exact way. But I know this listening mode will soon change, and all the words and mysteries will come pouring forth!! He, like his father before him, listens so intently when I talk-teach.) It was never lost on me that Michael was super smart from the beginning. I believed he understood EVERYTHING we talked about---that he processed EVERYTHING and that he was just as sure as I was that he could learn anything, do anything, and "be" anything that he wanted to be. I never changed my mind about this scenario, and while others seemed astounded and in awe about his "gifts," he and I just took them in stride.

One day when he was barely 2 years old, we were driving his dad's Gran Prix---Michael's car seat firmly in place behind the driver's seat. I could see him in the rearview mirror---Michael started talking to me—just a regular almost-2- year old conversation until I heard him say, "Mom, see my reflection?" I nearly drove the car off the road, but I remained cool and asked, "Where, Michael?" I saw him point to my rearview mirror and say, "That's Michael's reflection right there." While I had used the word "shadow" before with Michael, and we had played with our shadows while walking, I hadn't mentioned anything about "reflections" or what they were. So, this was pretty significant! He just was sharp that way---putting ideas together that were very advanced for his age.

When he was just a little guy---just a few months old---and in his play pen, Michael liked having little "toy stations"---a few toys placed strategically in each corner of the play pen. He would turn to "visit" each corner and babble to whoever or whatever was there. He especially liked to "talk" to "Swivel Head" and Raggedy Andy; and there was also a stack of colorful blocks which caught his attention, too. He was busy from day 1—taking it all in and relishing his place in this world.

We had to move out of the first apartment we shared together---Ed's apartment from his bachelor days at Lakeshore Apts. in Lake Park. This was because the apartment was only a one bedroom apartment, and Michael needed his own room for all his toys!! (Plus, his crib was a very tight squeeze in our bedroom!) Once we moved to the 2 bedroom apartment in the same complex, the 3 of us began to make and savor so many wonderful memories. One very early morning before he was 9 or 10 months old and not walking yet, Michael decided that he wanted to get to all his toys that weren't in his crib but all the way across the room. He must have pulled himself up then over the wooden slates of his crib and somehow lowered himself to the floor! We knew once Michael did something, he would repeat it. We had to try to make his crib safe. Ed rigged something to place over the top of the crib, but I hated it worse than Michael did! It looked like some kind of cage. So, as often happened throughout Michael's life, we accepted the miracle of him and his inquisitiveness and cleverness, took off the "crib lid" and just lowered the side of his crib so he could get out more easily when he chose to in order to explore. This worked out fine for him and for us. Sometimes he would crawl into our room, pull himself up, and tickle me until I woke up to play---sometimes this happened as early as 5:00 am! He began walking during the end of or beginning of his 9th or 10th month.

Michael was happiest when he was exploring or playing or "reading." He had such focus!! He never lost his incredible ability to focus on a task—no matter what that task asked of him. He could sit and "read" for long periods of time—concentrating on the same book until he was finished. He delighted in making up games as he crawled then later toddled throughout the apartment. He loved to create things, especially the pictures he drew and/or colored for his Nana Godwin and his Grandma and Grandpa Yonkers in Massachusetts. He loved to line up his stuffed animals along the wall in the hallway that led to the front door. Maybe they were there to greet any visitors (?) or to welcome daddy when he came home from work (?); or maybe he placed them there to protect us? Only Michael knew the answer to this.

One memory—a lasting one—happened when Michael was sick and his doctor prescribed Triaminc Syrup (orange flavored) for his bad cough. The first time I gave this medicine to him, he was sitting on his change table next to his crib. He took the medicine then spewed it out with such incredible force that it landed all the way over on the opposite side of the room, spraying the wall and a few toys in the process.

We never gave him that medicine again. He was only a few months old, but he already knew how to let us know what he could not take! Miracle indeed!

I remember Michael's first Christmas---yes, like it was yesterday! He was so inquisitive about all the decorations but especially about the Christmas tree. He would stare at the tree for long moments, and it looked like he was contemplating what a crazy idea it was to have a tree in the apartment. He wanted to touch everything, and I let him—teaching him "gently touch"---which he did. He really liked the ornament he had helped pick out—the little tennis boy who held his own tennis racquet—which was the first of many ornaments we bought and made for him each year. He also liked his Raggedy Andy ornament, liking it to hang at the bottom of the tree so he could find it and touch it easily. We made ornaments from the felt animals on his crib mobile when he was 2, and we even made (some would joke) ugly stocking heads---one for each of us---mom, Michael, dad and Shara. Of course there were computer ornaments, nature ornaments, cars, trains, trucks and animals like bears that marked and mimicked his growing up styles---ornaments that reflected his likes and loves. We made ornaments out of old Christmas cards, shells, sticks and pinecones—all things that we had collected over the year---and we always made enough of these ornaments for family and friends, many of whom grew to look forward to receiving these "specially made" presents. Michael liked making things for people---he liked the smiles he got from family and friends and teachers when he handed them their special, hand-made gifts. He was so pleased with his accomplishment but even more pleased with their reactions!

Of course Christmas was always the most exciting of all the holidays for Michael—gift-wise anyway—but he also loved the ceremony and fun when he was able to help light the Chanukah candles. He loved all the games, especially the Dreidel games. What a poignant, happy time we had—Ed and I—when Michael brought Laura and Viktor to our house in December of 2008—Viktor's first Chanukah—to light the candles for Chanukah, and we all said the Hebrew

Prayer as Michael lit the candles with Viktor.

Michael was so much fun to watch each Christmas. He really showed his pleasure and unabashed delight as each of his presents was revealed. But he insisted that we each open something, too---and he would wait until we did so. Holidays---especially Christmas---were grand and glorious times for us. According to Nana Godwin, we "spoiled" our kids, buying them way too many toys and other things. Ha! That was just what I had planned to do all along because, really, how can you possibly spoil a miracle??

Michael did not like loud noises. I think this dislike for loud noises began when we were living in the "Green" house—that was the house on Palm Road in West Palm Beach. (This was the way Michael and Shara identified the houses in which we lived—through their color schemes.) Michael was about 19 months old when we moved into our first home. The next door neighbor to our east parked his rather large boat on the side of his house, which happened to be within a few feet of Michael's and our bedrooms. The neighbor would return home late from a day of boating, back his boat into the parking area, spend time in and around the boat, spotlights glaring, then finally, usually late at night, turn on the very loud engine in order to clean it out! Michael would be scared awake, shaking, shivering and whimpering. This happened on most weekends but also during the week. We tried to reason with the neighbor—after all, he had 2 little children of his own-but there was no getting through to him. We let our hedge grow high and thick—a cherry hedge—hoping it would block some of the noise, but the chain link fence and hedge were no match for an engine that was run in between two concrete block houses, thus echoing even more loudly than an engine would while running on water. We installed black-out shades which took care of the very bright lights, but the noise remained a problem until we were able to move away from the neighborhood. I began to notice that Michael would become very nervous around this same time when he was faced with new environments or activities. I began to prepare him for things that would or might happen any time we went out. Also, we gave him his own flashlight to help him feel more secure at night. And many the nights I would walk down the hallway to check on him, and I would find him under his sheet—in bed—with the flashlight shining brightly. Much to my surprise, I didn't discover what he was doing until he reached the <u>Funk and Wagnal</u> "D" encyclopedia!! He had settled in to "read" those encyclopedias—one at a time—and didn't stop until he got to the last one---years later. He became a "night person" at a very young age. He just didn't seem to need the amount of sleep most kids his age required. Of course, he made up for this loss of sleep when he became a teenager!!

As a toddler, many times Michael would walk out to the family room where Ed and I would be sitting and watching TV---I was almost always exhausted from being with him all day and really needed some "adult" time---but he wasn't having any of that. Nana Godwin said I should be firm and take him back to bed---which I tried to do despite the myriad of questions he lobbed at me. Grandma Yonkers informed me that Ed did the same thing---she got the impression that Ed was afraid he would miss out on something----I think this was true of Michael, too.

Interestingly enough, as an adult, Michael became super involved with cars and engines and even raced Camaros (his own) at Moroso race track in PBG—thus overcoming any lingering fear from his youth that he had over loud noises.

When we were still living at our second Lakeshore Apartment, I used to take Michael for long bike rides---he rode in a special seat that Ed attached to the back of my bike—right behind my seat. We "talked" about everything and always stopped on the bridges, especially the low one on Northlake Blvd., so we could look into the water and search for boats, butterflies, frogs, and fish of all kinds. Later, when Michael was walking—at about 10 months or so-- he used to like to walk down the 2 flights of stairs outside and at the end of our building---then take a very long walk on the sidewalk. He always had his hat on for these walks---Dr. Anspach used to call him "the kid with the lid" because he never went anywhere without his hat! He was, after all, a true "toe-head"---for the first year or so he had white-blonde hair—and I was afraid for him to get too much sun. (I know this is hard to believe for those who knew Michael as an adult—his hair was jet black most days!) It turns out that I wasn't such an anal-retentive about this sun issue as it has become the "norm" now to protect ourselves from the sun's dangerous rays! Michael also wore his own sunglasses---Joe Cool we called him, and he even had a Joe Cool t-shirt –given to him by Cathie Wenderoth—it was his favorite Snoopy t-shirt. When we went out, I would dress him in his over-all shorts with a matching shirt and socks, his 2-toned sneakers (blue and white), and , of course, the inevitable hat—white to match.

Dr. Anspach was the doctor who finally helped us "fix" Michael's severe club feet. We had tried to get help from other doctors for this problem, but it was Dr. Anspach who was able to resolve Michael's feet problems. The little guy endured a number of cast changes to his feet and lower legs that first year of his life. Later on, we always credited the good doctor with helping Michael become the champion swimmer that he was—at both Jupiter Middle School and at Jupiter High School. His feet worked perfectly---like large flippers! What a pleasure it was to watch him swim---his first "win" happened at a meet at the North Palm Beach Country Club. He was either 6 or 7, and he "beat" Jack Nicklaus' son, Michael, also 6 or 7! Imagine the pride Ed felt—his son had bested The Golden Bear's son in athletics! Of course, I was on the side lines doubled over in hysteria, laughing so hard at the sight of this "race" which was pretty much a stop and go event! Between giggles, we cheered the "racers" on to the other side of the pool and back again. It was a very long race!

Many years later we would watch in wonder as Michael swam and won a place at the FL State championships—more than one time—despite the fact that he swam against future Olympic breaststrokers from Spanish River High School. He was a talented, gifted swimmer who didn't even swim and train year round as the other champions did. Even Beth Howard, his extraordinary high school coach, couldn't believe he had such ability with seemingly so little effort. Well, he was our miracle baby after all!

While Michael was certainly our miracle, it became clear that we, his parents, weren't quite up to his standards of excellence in this same regard! If I haven't already mentioned it, Michael had a wonderfully dry sense of humor---even as a young boy---that he practiced using at all times---always making his father and I laugh at the most unexpected times. When he was about 15 years old and lying on the family room oval-braided rug at Trailwood—and watching the TV, an announcement came on to say that Burt Reynolds and Loni Anderson were adopting a baby boy---to be named Quinton. A friend of ours had already informed us of this pending adoption----having a vested interest in the couple. But I had not revealed any of this privileged information because we were adoptive parents ourselves and did not want to contribute to interfering with their right to privacy---in order that the adoption process would go smoothly. While I always told Michael (and, later, Shara) that 2 women had grown each of them in their tummies for daddy and me (and wasn't that nice of them?), I was secretly afraid that the biological parents would come to their senses and ask to have our 2 miracles returned to them! I did not want this scenario to happen to any adoptive parents, especially high-profile ones like the Reynolds'.

Of course Ed and I had a contingency plan if the biological parents ever tried to gain custody of our babies. We would fly to Australia and hide out there! Anyway, after the announcement about Quinton's adoption by Burt and Loni, Michael swiveled his head back, looked straight at me, and said, "Oh sure!! Where were THEY 15 years ago 'cause they sure missed out on getting this GIFT!" What a sense of humor he had! (How could parents like us compete with the likes of the handsome Burt Reynolds and the beautiful Loni Anderson?)

Later on, after Michael had met and fell in love with his Laura, he mentioned that Laura wanted to search his biological background---with which we heartily agreed. We always thought that having our children's medical histories was, at the very least, a most important tool—helpful to them and for any grandchildren that we might have! But Michael informed us that he wasn't interested in knowing anything about his biological family because it could turn out that they were "as screwed up as Burt and Loni were!" (This idea stemmed from the fact that the Reynolds had divorced.) I think Michael was trying, in his own way, to tell us that we weren't such bad parents after all!

Exercising was always a part of our lives as a family. When Michael was a little guy, not even a year old, he would sit in his orange Umbroller Stroller with his tennis whites on---the matching ones I made for him and his dad---and his ever-present white hat. In his little hands he held a zip-lock baggie full of Peanut Butter Captain Crunch cereal, and he would sit munching and watching for hours while his dad and I played tennis. The courts were just a little south of and on the same street as our apartment in Lake Park---they were located in Kelsey Park which sat just west of the beautiful Inlet Waterway---there was always a wonderful breeze coming off the water. Michael was so patient---and a great audience for us---clapping and making noises whenever he felt we deserved his attention! He certainly amazed everyone else who was in and around the park. No one could believe this little guy would sit and watch so patiently while we played a few games of tennis. Of course he always biked with me –or if Ed was home, Michael would sit in his seat behind daddy while I ran alongside of them.

Years later when my knees complained of the running, I switched to biking, and many times Michael would ride his bike with me—pushing me to go faster. I enjoyed riding 5 miles a day, and riding a bike was made easier after we moved into the house Michael helped to build—Trailwood Circle—this was made easier because the circle was a mile around. We also walked—"a lot!"

When Michael was in the 6th grade at Allamanda Elementary School in Palm Beach Gardens, he should have been selected to be a Safety Patrol in his first semester. But he had had a run-in (as did I) with the teacher who was in charge of the patrol program at Allamanda, and she decided that he wouldn't be able to become a patrol until the second semester---thus keeping him from being able to go on the coveted Washington, DC Patrol Train Trip. (That teacher was a very confrontational type person. She made many mistakes in the classroom—among other things--regarding grammar and spelling, and unfortunately, Michael became very frustrated and tried to correct some of those mistakes. Of course she did not like that at all. And eventually the administration decided that a move to another teacher's classroom would resolve the problem and would be the best thing to do in Michael's best interests. And he thrived in Mr. Marder's classroom, using and building upon his ever-increasing computer skills, skills that helped shape who and what he became later in life---a successful adult entrepreneur. I found over the years that there are many teachers who have a difficult time dealing with and relating to gifted kids in the classroom because these teachers wouldn't or couldn't accept the fact that gifted kids are most times brighter than those of us who teach them!)

Anyway, Michael's dad and I decided to take him and his sister on that trip to Washington DC. We had a marvelous time---Michael and I made dad and Shara walk all over Washington---and I do mean everywhere. We had a wonderful time seeing and exploring things the Patrols would never see—and things they would see. We got to see exactly where Lincoln and JFK lay after they were assassinated (in the very bowels of the Capitol Building) before they were placed in the Capitol—lying in State--for all the mourners to view. (I connected with a guard in the Capitol—we shared an interest in certain reading material—so he took us to places other tourists would not have been allowed to see.) And after this experience, we went to Senator

Lawton Childs' office ---Michael sat in the Senator's huge chair after being invited into the office by Senator Childs' very accommodating secretary; we visited the White House (where President Ronald Reagan presided); we went to the Senate and House Chambers and saw where the legislators actually debated all of our country's laws; and we even got to ride on the very private underground subway beneath the offices of the Senators and House Representatives—we were invited to do so by an Ohio Senator (Senator Howard Metzembaum(D). This was a glorious vacation for all of our family.

As Michael became an active teenager, exercising with his mom wasn't such a cool thing to do anymore. But at least he let me cheer him on while he swam for the Jupiter High Warrior Swim team!!

Michael was an extraordinary Boy Scout. When he first joined Jerry Perkins' Troop 751, he was immediately whisked away to an extended weekend camping trip in the Keys. I was really scared to let our little boy go away on a trip with virtual "strangers." The "what ifs" formed a solid wall of questions in my mind, and my imagination began to "see" too many possibilities, none of which were very positive. We prayed we were making the right decision as we packed Michael's things in his back pack; we included in his back pack numerous stamped envelopes all addressed to us, explaining to him that he could write to us if he needed anything at all. Of course we included our phone number and instructions on how to call us. My fear factor went into overdrive when we received a collect call from the Keys—just shortly after he would have arrived there---I literally saw us speeding to the Keys to rescue our suffering son. But Michael came on the line and said, in a calm but irritated voice, "Could you please send me my bathing suit---we forgot to pack it?!" A loud "WHEW" emanated from my mouth after we hung up---rather quickly, too----because he couldn't talk long as they were off in the canoe to go exploring in the crystal clear waters of the Gulf of Mexico! Suffice it to say, he was having a marvelous time camping; Jerry was a wonderful man and Troop Leader, and Michael really took to camping in tents with his new Boy Scout friends. We never did receive even one letter from him---he was too busy making memories. (I am reminded that when I was a Girl Scout and attended summer camp, I endured spiders and roaches in our cabins, stinky outside outhouses, showers with walls but no roof, and terrible, inedible food---with the exception of Apple Butter (on the tables for every meal), and I would write to my parents every single day, letting them know just how much I was suffering!)

Michael fell in love with every aspect of Scouts and camping. This was a life right up his alley, and he became an expert at all of it---cooking, fire-making, setting up his tent and camp site, and respecting nature and all it had to offer. I remember one time when he was staying up at the Tanakeeta Boy Scout Camp in Tequesta; the other boys found a black snake and were throwing rocks and sticks at it, cutting it severely. Michael insisted on bringing that snake home with us that summer, and we nursed the snake back to good health --- each day we put hydrogen peroxide on the area that was cut. "Blackie" lived in an old terrarium we had---we kept him on our back screened-in porch. I drew the line at letting the snake stay inside the house----and even if I didn't, Michael's dad would have moved out if a snake had been allowed to take up residence inside our house!

Michael's tender-heartedness toward living things was most evident throughout his life. When we let the now healthy black snake free, he paid us back for Michael's quality care by staying in our outside gardens, patrolling and getting rid of all the "bad" snakes like the pigmy rattlers and the coral snakes! We never saw those "bad" snakes again thanks to "Blackie." Of course Shara and I would be <u>very</u> startled as we worked in our gardens---especially in the Zinnia garden in front of our house at Trailwood---because "Blackie" would pop his head up to say "hello" as we were working.

Michael would have other fabulous Boy Scout Leaders through the years. Jim and Lorraine White---and their entire, incredible family---were certainly most dedicated to making the

Scouting experience everything it could be. They took over Troop 751 when Jerry Perkins needed to step down. Michael's scouting career culminated when both he and his dad were selected for the Order of the Arrow---and finally, when Michael completed his Eagle Scout path.

Michael "let" me play with him for longer than most kids would. We did a lot of hiking through our "woods", especially in Trailwood---we liked the ones across the lake where the little pier for fishing stood until the wooden pathway had to be removed because the wood had rotted. We still went into those "woods." We liked to skate, too, and skated all around our very accommodating circular cement driveway and around all of Trailwood. (I had to stop the outdoor skating when one day I took a bad fall and broke some ribs. I put a belt around me, went inside, lay down and took it easy for a few days. I never told anyone about my ribs---Michael would have been worried about hurting himself. He sometimes reacted in fear over something that should just be a minor issue---once he had a splinter in his finger and ran from me refusing to allow me to get it out—he did suffer from some irrational fears.)

Michael also liked to play baseball in what was an empty lot next door to us. One day this lot would become Officer Nicholson's family home. Michael always included me in the baseball games---always as the pitcher. Of course, I was in charge of keeping that empty lot mowed---getting rid of all the pesky weeds that could grow as tall as Michael! We also played tennis against our two-car garage door---and had to promise dad that we would paint the garage door when it got marked up with too many tennis ball shadows. But I think the "sport" I loved the best was when I got to just watch Michael doing anything---he was fabulous at everything he tried---even hitting golf balls from our front yard in Trailwood----he'd hit them into the lake across the street. His dad secretly harbored the idea that Michael would one day want to play golf with him, but Michael never developed any desire to play golf. I think the sport of golf moved too slowly for him---he loved speed in all things! When we built his own half pipe for his skate-boarding pleasure, it was so big it took 3 people to drag it down the driveway and into the street so he could use it. We constantly prayed that no cars would come down the road while he was using it! He was a fabulous skateboarder. Kids came from all around—even other neighborhoods to watch him and to learn from him. He perfected many tricks with his skate board. He was focused, skillful, talented, and did everything with incredible poise and smoothness. His adaptation to sports was pure miracle and beauty combined!

Michael wasn't really a competitive person except when he was going up against himself. He always wanted to do a little better the next time. But there was one time when he **really** wanted to win. He was at Boy Scout camp, and his troop had never won the Wednesday Family Night Bake-off. He really wanted his troop to win this award---so he called me to ask if I would enter the contest---others had tried but failed in years past. Shara and I said "yes" to this challenge, and we came up with a brilliant idea---we told Michael we would be sure to win, especially with our "suck up" idea. We went out and bought the biggest and best tasting cheesecake we could find; then we made chocolate icing and put it in a homemade cake decorator bag and "drew" the Boy Scout emblem on the top of the cheesecake. Since it was the older leaders and administrators who judged and ate the Bake-off entries, we were not surprised when Shara and I had our names called out as the # 1 winners of that year's Bake-off contest! Michael was so pleased for his troop---they finally won the coveted WNF Bake-off! And a very important life's lesson was learned by Michael and Shara that night: Always give 'em what you know they want, and you'll always come out on top!

Michael was an extraordinary student pretty much all through his life. There were "bumps" along the way, but he usually rose to the top---or, at least, succeeded in his educational mission. Many of his teachers would tell his dad and me that he was the best student, the brightest, the cleverest, the most creative, the one with the most humor, and the most likeable student they had ever had in their classrooms. His classroom successes began at the Hinton's (Mary and Jim) home then later at their Professional Learning Center in Jupiter. Because Mary and Jim were good friends, we couldn't take what those teachers at PLC said too seriously. But we soon learned that it was all too true.

When I had to go back to work, I begged Mary to take our 2 kids into her home---the center was not opened yet but was being built. Thank goodness she did---despite the fact that she was pregnant with Catie (her second daughter). She took our 2 and a couple of other children whose parents were also desperate for quality child care. The drive from our house in southwestern Palm Beach County to Jupiter was a long one---at least an hour back then. Ed would drive them up to Mary's house, and I would pick them up. I had to report to Palm Beach Gardens High for work early, but I got out earlier then Ed did. This arrangement worked out quite well until we were finally able to sell our house on Palm Road and move to rent a home on Loxahatchee Drive in Jupiter.

The school was finally finished, and the kids and Mary took up classroom residence at Professional Learning Center. Bonnie Waluda, who became a very close friend, was Michael's "foundation" teacher. She taught him to read and was a wonderful influence on him. Her sense of humor, her intelligence, and her sense of fairness helped shape Michael into the extraordinary student and human being he became.

In first grade Michael attended a well regarded private religious school---I was the designated driver who picked him up after school--along with Curry Hinton and 2 other children--and I drove them home to Jupiter. The children were taken to school by Mary and others. Michael didn't stay long at this school even though his teacher, Miss J--, was a lovely and competent teacher. Michael, she told us, was way ahead of everyone else in his classroom and always finished his work ahead of all the others. So Miss J-- made what I think was a sensible decision----she engaged him as her "helper", and he helped his fellow classmates to learn how to do the work. Well, one day, I received a call from the school's principal in which she informed me that she was going to have to discipline Michael by paddling him. I quickly responded, "Do not touch him. I am on my way over to the school." When I arrived, the principal explained that Michael was "a cheater", and they did not tolerate cheaters at their school. I turned to Michael and asked him the following, "Do you know what a cheater is?" Scared to death, he quickly answered, "No, mom." I then asked Michael to explain to me what had happened. He said, "We were taking a test, and I finished first. "Ricky" (name changed) turned to me and asked me for an answer. I tried to be a helper so that he could answer the question." Case closed for me, but the principal insisted that he needed to be taught a lesson, and she was going to paddle him. I took Michael with me, and we went back to his classroom to collect all of his things. He said goodbye to his classmates while I had a chat with Miss J--. I told her if she ever was lucky enough to have another student with Michael's skills, she should be careful to explain the difference between being a "helper" and being a "cheater." Michael learned fast---he never "helped" anyone again on a test. And he certainly was an incredible test-taker. He took the SAT once as an eleventh grader, scoring in the 1200's---with an almost perfect math score (700's). The perfect score on an SAT test at that time was a 1600. Of course anyone who scores well on any standardized test is a miracle to me!!

When Michael began attending Allamanda Elementary School, he was immediately tested and placed in the gifted program. This school really handled this program in the right way as far as I was concerned because he was able to have the opportunity to be in regular classes, too. His classes were accelerated in some subjects and all students were pulled out for "specials"---in his case this meant going to Miss Stant and Mrs. Craddock for gifted instruction a few times a week—or daily? There were many wonderful things that happened in that Gifted Class, but even more wonderful things happened after school. One very special opportunity had to do with the game of chess. Miss Stant wanted her students to become accomplished chess players. She engaged a good friend of hers to come in to work with the kids who stayed after school---kids who were eager to learn more chess strategies. Carmine Nigro was a delightful little man---so soft spoken but very serious about teaching the intricacies of chess to children. He even placed me at a board to hone my minimal chess skills! Imagine our astonishment when we learned that Carmine Nigro had been the chess teacher to Bobby Fisher, one of the most famous, albeit strangest, American Chess Champions of all time. It was Bobby who beat the Russian Chess Champion, Boris Spasky, the champion who was supposedly unbeatable; and Bobby's life was made into a major motion picture—*The Search for Bobby Fisher*.

Chess was important to Michael's dad---who played in high school and in college. Ed was so proud of his 2 kids---playing chess with Carmine Nigro. (Years later, Ed and I would join hundreds of people at the Gardens Mall in Palm Beach Gardens to play chess against the famous Chess Grand Master Susan Polgar. Now I went down after 14 plays, but Ed held his own and was one of a very few left playing---after hours and hours---and he did NOT lose to the Grand Master. She offered him a draw—1 of 11 to attain this prestigious status. She lost 2 or 3 games out of the hundreds she played simultaneously that day; this was done in order to earn a Guinness World Record, which she did!) Michael was very proud of his dad!!

Ed and Susan Polgar

Because Michael was in gifted programs throughout his elementary, middle school, and high school years, one of the on-going requirements in elementary school was that he had to participate each year in the Science Fair by completing a science project. Of all the projects he cleverly constructed, the one I was most impressed by was his robot. He built the robot out of a rounded cylindrical Quaker Oats cereal box; the yellow lids from cans of Hershey Chocolate Syrup (to be cut out to form perfect glasses); wire; and the parts from different toys to give the robot wheels and for the motorized part of the robot. He also made the remote control for his robot---he found a small, silver box used for holiday presents and fashioned a perfect controller. He won a Blue Ribbon at the fair that year and was interviewed by a local TV station personality. One of the most important parts of the competition was the Judges' interviews. These interviews took place so that the Judges could discern if the students really understood their projects enough to explain them in depth---thus proving that the students—not the daddies—had done the work on their science projects. Michael impressed those Judges with his knowledge and understanding of how to build and successfully make a working robot that would move by remote control--- and it is interesting to note that this project was completed back in the early 1980's when we did not have computers or internet access to this kind of information.

We dubbed his robot "The Professor" because after looking at him with his large, yellow spectacles, we decided he was different and needed something more to set him apart from all the other robots. Michael fashioned a mortarboard for him out of black construction paper. The robot's glasses begged to be accompanied by this hat of a graduate! And he certainly did "look" very intelligent.

Michael was the consummate "hugger." I mean there has never been ANYONE and there is NOBODY whom I know--or have ever met--who could or can give a hug like Michael could. You felt so much from his hug---you felt safety, love, and compassion. His was not some wishy-washy hug that left you feeling empty or that seemed more of an obligation than a true representation of loving feelings toward the one being hugged. No, when Michael hugged me, I felt cherished and loved. His was an all encompassing hug, and his approval "growl" that accompanied the hug made me feel even more content and loved. His hugs lasted, too---I never wanted to be the one to break away from his hug, but if I didn't, I am convinced he would have hugged me forever! I didn't want to be selfish as his dad was always waiting for his hug from Michael. Yet, when Michael and Ed finished their hug, invariably I would sneak in for another, quicker one, and it was like Michael expected me to do this---even encouraged me to do it by putting out his left hand and arm---reaching for me. I wonder if anyone else ever noticed this wonderful talent and skill Michael showed to us. Shara has mentioned it to me—his sister recognized his expert hugging ability!

It meant a great deal to me to know that he liked hugging me (and his dad)---that he felt this genuine affection and showed it through his incredible hugs. I would like to think he learned this as a small boy because Ed and I could never help ourselves. We LOVED to hug our miracle children----Michael and Shara both "endured" enveloping kinds of bear hugs from us throughout their youth and into their adulthood.

All their lives, I did and still will always look at them and think "What a miracle that each of them came to live with us---how very lucky can one woman and one man be????!!" Now the challenge is on for Viktor----I'll bet a bag of pop-corn that he'll be the next, best, great hugger, and I'm waiting in line for my hug!

Michael was around 4 years old, and we were still living in the Green house---the one on Palm Road in West Palm Beach. (Remember, Michael and, later, Shara identified the houses we lived in by their color schemes—the trim color. The house we rented on Loxahatchee Drive in Jupiter was the Yellow house. We built what I refer to as my "dream" house in Trailwood, and the kids reverently referred to this house as the "Trailwood" house or the Brown house. Whatever its name, it was truly a special house in which to live---with its 40 by 20 foot pool and its large-sized rooms.)

Anyway, Michael had been invited to a couple of sleepovers. One invitation was from Jennifer Watson. John and Lana Watson were our very good friends—I grew up on the same street in West Palm Beach with Lana—and their youngest daughter, Jennifer, was about 2 months younger than Michael and was one of his good friends. Another sleepover he was invited to go to was at Boomer Petti's house—this one was an all boy sleepover. Because Michael continued to have a problem at night---he was what they called a bed-wetter---I told him that he would probably need to wear a diaper at night on the sleepovers so that nobody woke up wet in the morning. This mortified him! He wasn't having any of that diaper stuff---but he certainly understood why it would be necessary---he didn't want his friends getting all wet and being "grossed out" by it! He knew "Aunt" Lana and "Aunt" Sara were fine with whatever he decided and would do whatever he wanted----but he didn't want to sleep in a separate bed, either. So, he chose to stay home and not go on the sleepovers---a difficult choice for a 4 year old to make! One morning, he came to me and said, "Mom, I'm the only one who gets the bed wet. Even Shara doesn't get her bed wet. Is there something I can do to make it stop?" I called our Pediatrician, Dr. John Green, and was told, "Oh, don't worry about it. He'll outgrow it---and don't make a big deal out of it or he'll feel guilty!" Well, we were **not** making a big deal out of it. After all, he wasn't doing it on purpose. Because Michael was insisting on some help, I decided to call and make an appointment with the newer doctor who had joined Dr. Green's practice—Dr. Stuart Babcock. Dr. Babcock just happened to be Mary Hinton's very good friend, and I wanted to get his opinion about what, if anything could be done to help Michael. I made the appointment—on a day when I knew Dr. Greene would be out of the office—and we entered Dr. Babcock's exam room and met him for the first time. He was kind of shy and quietly-spoken with me, but he wasn't with Michael. They engaged in a lengthy conversation---one in which the doctor was able to coax Michael into telling him what was bothering him. A very relaxed Michael (to relax was very unusual for Michael to do in a doctor's office) explained to Doctor B that he felt "different" and wanted to be like all his friends and even his little sister—he did not want to wet his bed anymore, and he asked Dr. Babcock if he could please "fix" him. Doctor B told him about a company that went around the country and helped kids just like Michael---and he asked if he would like to meet the people. Michael said, "YES!" then asked, "Why do I do this when my friends don't?" The doctor explained that Michael's sleep cycle---the way he fell asleep and slept in the night---was not working as it should, and it would need to be changed----this would "fix" the problem. Michael told the doctor he was ready to "change his cycle." So, the doctor gave us all the information, we called the company, and set up a meeting with one of their representatives. The gentleman came to our home----on time---fortunately for him as Michael stood waiting at the front living-room windows and would have told the man "You're late!" as he was wearing his "real boy" watch and knew the exact time of their appointment. The man was very competent at what he did, explaining how Michael would be sleeping on a large, square screen which would be attached to a battery operated buzzer; the buzzer would sound off with a loud buzz the instant the screen sensed moisture, and this would awaken Michael---and his parents--- and allow us the opportunity to take Michael to the bathroom. The man took Michael out to his car (while his dad and I watched nervously at the windows----I had completely lost sight of the fact that this meeting had been set up by us after receiving a trusted doctor's recommendation! I stood there thinking, "Please God, don't let this guy be a kidnapper who goes around stealing kids---maybe taking them back to their biological parents who would pay big money to get them back! While the children were little, we lived in constant fear that this could happen.)

So, we began this program---Michael taking charge almost immediately. He picked out his own screen and cover. Dad did all the business end of this deal, and I kept the daily journals making note of the progress---both success and lack thereof---of the program. Dad would call the company I think twice a week to give a report on all the statistics I had gathered. The company would make suggestions---changing the levels on the screen. As the weeks went by, Michael slowly began to make progress, and he told me that he just wanted his dad to come with him at night now "'cause we're both boys and you're not." I think he was letting me know that he was joining a club I could never be a part of because I "went to the bathroom sitting down!" And, he was now no longer wetting his bed every night and didn't want anything to interfere with his success.

And finally, the day came when Michael helped to box up the late-night contraption that had helped him change his sleep-cycle and had enabled him to stop wetting his bed. Imagine his beautiful lit-up face with a smile a mile wide as he walked out the front door carrying his packed suitcase, on his way to his first sleep-over!! He had a right to be proud of himself because even before he turned 4, he had taken control of an important part of his life and overcome a difficult situation that had made him feel "different." He learned he COULD control his destiny no matter how difficult or seemingly insurmountable a problem appeared to be.

Of course after the fact, we learned that many boys---some who became famous as adults like Michael Landon (of *Little House on the Prairie* fame) had suffered with the same problem; and some of these boys were humiliated by parents and family who did not or could not try to understand that their boys were not wetting their beds on purpose. Can you see why we view Michael as our miracle? A little boy turned his life in the direction he chose for it to go—made adult decisions---that makes him a miracle!

Michael's desire to have his own dog seemed to be his single focus one summer. While he had continued to ask us if he could have his own dog, he became resigned to the fact that we couldn't have one because of his life-threatening allergies. But this one summer he was just a little boy who desperately wanted and needed a pet---one that didn't have to be buried within a few months of being brought home to live with us, or flushed down the toilet before Michael realized that the floating-on-top goldfish was no longer with us! This one summer day we were swimming at "Aunt" Janie's house---with Jackie---at the 36th Street house in West Palm Beach when Janie announced that we needed to go pay a visit to her friend, Maile. Maile and her wonderful family---lots of sweet kids---just lived a block or so away in a lovely big house. We walked there with all our kids in tow, bathing suits drying in the warm sunshine. What we found when we got there was a menagerie of animals---all kinds---guinea pigs, gerbils, hamsters, rabbits, of course cats, and the necessary dog or 2. We were there because the gerbils had given birth to a ton of babies, and Maile thought Jackie, Michael, and Shara might be interested in adopting one. Michael was just beside himself with joy, I was in shock, Shara wanted a bunny, and Ed was going to have to get used to feeding and housing another family member. It took Michael a very long time to pick out just the right gerbil (they all looked the same to me—little hairy rats!) And when he found just the perfect gerbil, we took "Whiskers" (who would in later years become somewhat of a newspaper celebrity!) home with us, taking time to stop and purchase all the necessary accoutrements for a gerbil. While the wheel was a very important and integral part of Whiskers' daily life, we soon discovered that he much preferred home-made wood chunk blocks that were a little larger than Lincoln Logs---and he preferred the homemade ones to the pet store ones. He REALLY liked the empty toilet paper rolls the best---he would bite them into little tiny pieces and make his nest with them in the just-purchased terrarium we later used for Blackie---the rescued black snake from Boy Scout Camp.

Whiskers' cage had to be cleaned once a week---by his owner, Michael---and new cedar chips had to be placed in the dried out and cleaned terrarium, and his water bottle had to be emptied and the old water replaced with fresh water. That water bottle had to be totally replaced about 10 times in Whiskers' lifetime because he had "teeth of steel"---he literally nibbled his way through the steel bottom--thus allowing his cage to be flooded!! Of course as all gerbil owners do, we learned a whole lot about these pets---one thing was that they HAD to continually chew or their teeth would grow way too long! We had also bought a big plastic exercise ball for Whiskers (we couldn't let him get "bored" or out of shape!!) We would place Whiskers in the ball----especially while his cage was being cleaned when he first came to live with us at the Trailwood home. Later, he would sit on Michael's shoulder or in his shirt pocket and watch as his "dad" cleaned his cage! He could certainly roll all over the house in that ball---and he didn't even hurt himself or get lost. One of us usually kept an eye on him. He would crash and careen into the walls and the furniture and just have a great time rolling around his domain. Michael trained him so well that he could take Whiskers out of his cage, and the gerbil would never try to escape from Michael. Michael would be on his bed with Whiskers, reading or doing homework, and Whiskers would just be running up and down right next to Michael. Whiskers most loved to ride on Michael's shoulder—inside the house and out----and he would give Michael little kisses on his ear or cheek as they went! Whiskers learned to stop biting us at a very early age---I forget exactly how we accomplished this, but I remember being very patient and tapping Whiskers on his little rump each time he tried to bite. He learned quickly and never bit anyone ever again after our "training" sessions! I wasn't surprised at our being able to make this happen----Michael was always working miracles in his life. We buried Whiskers 6 or 7 years later, with full honors, in a very solemn ceremony. We knew he was dying as he had a tumor that grew. But Whiskers didn't want to go---at least not until Michael could let him go. One school night, I told Michael that I thought Whiskers might really be suffering---he lay in his cage rarely moving, he wasn't eating much at all, and he had lost much of his body weight. I asked Michael if he could tell Whiskers that it was okay if Whiskers wanted to go to heaven. Michael said he could; he walked to the cage of his beloved pet and whispered that he could go if he needed to.

The next day when we returned home from school, we found Whiskers was no longer alive. Michael found the "perfect" box then found some beautiful velvet material—blue—amongst my sewing material, and he lovingly lined the box in that same velvet. Michael kissed Whiskers and gently placed him in the velvet-lined box then placed cotton balls all around Whiskers. He put the partially chewed wood block inside the box, too, along with some cedar chips. Michael selected a place to bury him, in front of the house by the garage—in the little garden there. He dug the hole, we stood there, Michael, Shara and I, while Michael said a sweet prayer of thanks for all the years we had with Whiskers and for giving us a pet who loved us so much!

There would be other pets in the coming years---another gerbil named Einstein (who did NOT live up to his namesake!), Blackie the rescued black snake, and of course there was Fluffy, Shara's nasty-cute hamster who bit everyone except her! As an adult, Michael owned an albino boa constrictor; and then after he was married, he finally got his dog---in fact 2 of them. Dooley and Bueller were their "dad's" best pets ever---they loved to play with Michael---Frisbee was (and still is) a favorite of both dogs. But hanging out with dad was really their favorite activity---and dad worked at home so there was a whole bunch of time for hanging with dad. Weimaraners are easy on people with allergies, and we have since learned that kids who are exposed to family pets from the beginning don't usually develop the terrible trouble with allergies like Michael had.

When Michael was a young teen, and we were still living in the Trailwood home, he used to love to go fishing in the lake in front of our house and across the street. One day he came back from the lake very excited---he had caught the biggest Big Mouth bass that the lake held. This was the fish that every neighbor who loved to fish talked about---the one Cliff Burg had had put into the lake when he had first stocked it---and it was the one fish that had eluded his own fishing pole for all the years we lived in Trailwood! So---here comes Michael up the driveway, a good-looking filled out teen, wearing a huge grin and shorts and flip-flops—no shirt as usual—and it is twilight. He calls to us, and we all file out to witness his miracle catch---he has caught the one fish that has NEVER been out of our lake since it was placed there. We take a picture of the proud fisherman with his catch---as Michael holds open the mouth just as wide as it would go—emphasizing the humongous width of this fish's mouth. Then Michael turned and quickly walked back to the lake and gently released that Big Mouth Bass. He was--and remained all his life--the generous fisherman who understood the concept of fishing for sport. He made sure the unharmed fish went back into the lake so that another fisherman would one day have the same opportunity that he had had----this display of teen sportsmanship is truly a miracle for it reveals that very special part of Michael--the selfless part of Michael. He wanted to share the thrill of catching this elusive fish with others.

20

When we were living in the Green House---the one on Palm road---we had a chain link fence with a gate out in the front of the west side of the house---right near the garage door. This fence went all around the back of our property and to the front of the eastern side of the property up to the front of the house---where Michael's and our bedrooms were located. We also had a Florida Cherry hedge alongside the fence---which we allowed to grow thicker and higher to afford us some privacy in the backyard and to further buffer the lights and noise that came late in the night from our neighbor with the boat and loud engine who lived to the east of us! On the west side of our house, the hedge ended in the back yard before the back edge of the house began. Even though we had a chain link fence on that side, we were still able to see into the next door neighbor's back yard. These neighbors were really very nice people---they had older daughters and 2 very cute dachshunds—Sunshine was the mom---but I forget the name of her puppy. Those two dogs were so precious. They loved Michael---if he was outside playing and they were also outside, they would stand on their side of the chain link fence and bark and jump up and down until Michael came over to say "hi." One day---Michael wasn't even 2 yet---we were out working in the backyard garden. We heard the dogs and Michael toddled over to say "hi" to them. When he didn't come back and I no longer heard the dogs, I got up from my gardening to check on him. And there he was—as I rounded the corner---hanging by his little fingers and tennis shoes at the top of the chain link fence trying to swing his leg up and over!!! I swallowed my fear and asked him—calmly, "What are you doing at the top of the fence, Michael?" He answered—just as calmly, "Sunshine needs me to play with her." I must say he made me feel kind of slow for not having figured that out on my own! I deftly removed him from the top of the fence and explained to him that we couldn't just climb the fence and go into Sunshine's yard without permission from Bill---Sunshine's "daddy." Immediately, Michael began to yell, "Bill—Can I come play with Sunshine?" Fortunately for me, Bill was at work and couldn't answer Michael's cry. But later---when we told him of Michael's escapade---he laughed and promised to steer him to the front door of his house. He also would tell Michael not to climb the fence anymore.

I must say, Michael didn't climb the fence as often as I thought he would after that, but he still kept his climbing skills up to par---we would find him at the top of the fence quietly talking to one or both of the dogs---or he would entertain his cousins, Dorrie and Barbie, by showing off his fast climbing skills as he climbed to the top of the fence with a huge smile on his face! Dorrie and Barbie lived just around the corner from us—the street north of ours—with Uncle Bob and Aunt Nancy. In fact Michael and Barbie share the same birthday—January 12th---but of course Barbie is a number of years older than Michael.

21

Okay! It's time to talk about the PBF---plastic bag family referred to in an earlier chapter. It seems that the Yonkers' family couldn't ever travel anywhere without quite a few plastic bags ---bags that held all our necessaries! One vacation to the water park at Bush Gardens in Tampa---Adventure Island---found us all carrying our change of clothes, shoes, towels and shampoo in to the park---using Publix plastic bags---while others walked in carrying fancy canvas bags full of their things! But, those Publix plastic bags were just perfect for carrying our wet suits, soggy towels and damp flip-flops at the end of the day! (We weren't aware at the time of the impact those bags were having on our environment—that plastic lasts forever in the waste and garbage fields of our world—but we know better now; we utilize far fewer plastic bags in traveling today—in fact we even reuse those same bags!) We really enjoyed those vacations spent at different water parks ---we "did" Wet 'N Wild in Orlando several times---and of course we went to the little water park in West Palm Beach (which is today a HUGE, cool, water park!); but our favorite water park by far was always Adventure Island. While Ed, Michael, and Shara dared to go down any and all of the tallest of water slides---even the give-you-a-wedgie ones---I could never talk myself into it. When we went to the natural water park at Disney World, Typhoon Lagoon, Michael finally coaxed me into going down the "high drop" slides in the pool area---they are the slides that suddenly stopped in mid air and dropped you about 40 or 50 feet into the pool. I loved it once I dared to try it, but my true fear was that someone would follow me down and land on me in the water---I was scared I would drown. Michael and Shara fixed that problem----she would go in front of me and Michael would always go after me. I trusted him to give me enough time to swim out of the way!! I did love all the swirly slides---they were not so high and gave me a more leisurely ride down.

In June of 2009, some of our family visited the water park at Cypress Gardens, and Shara talked me into going down the double tube, very high "swirly" slide---I did it in honor of Michael---once----with her. What a ride that was! The hardest part for me was climbing all the stairs to get to the top---I was truly winded—but the ride was well worth it.

Water parks weren't the only place that found us carrying our belongings in plastic bags. We once walked into the very exclusive Lincoln Hotel in Tampa, jauntily carrying our inevitable(?) plastic bags crammed full of our things. For the first time, Michael and Shara seemed a little embarrassed at the long stares we received from the other upscale hotel guests. As we rode up to our room in the glass elevator, I told the kids that they just had to think and act as if they were eccentrics---people who behaved in such a way that seemed odd or out of place to others but who were "accepted" or "forgiven" their eccentricities because of their vast wealth and/or their status in the world. And I told Michael to hold his head high and with pride as he was just as good and important as the family we had seen in the lobby who all sported Gucci luggage!!

Michael stepped out of the elevator and began walking in a sliding motion-- down the hotel hallway, carefully carrying his plastic bags well away from and parallel to his sides, with his face turned up and staring at the ceiling---all the way to our room!! He looked very "snooty", and he cracked us all up!!

There was also a trip to Washington DC—with plastic bags in tow--carrying our "stuff" to our hotel room—a room that was on a top floor of a very tall hotel, thus requiring each of us-- for a long period of time-- to look aloof and unfazed by the strange looks we were receiving from other guests; and there were trips to other hotels—hotels in Disney World; hotels in Tampa near Adventure Island; and in NY and MA--and for each of these trips, the Yonkers sported plastic bags; and in St. Augustine, the oldest city in the New World, we bravely swung our things in plastic bags; and plastic bags carried our things on trips to other FL tourist "hotspots." Wherever we traveled, we always included the very exclusive and eccentric Yonkers Family matching "luggage"---Publix plastic bags filled with our important "stuff"!!! And we still carry the PPBs* everywhere we travel---even to England!! We have to---because it's tradition!

(Note: In a bid to honor Michael's very environmentally savvy wife and to honor our fragile environment, we do utilize far fewer plastic bags now when we travel! And, we recycle!)

22

One thing I forgot to mention when we took our family "patrol" trip to Washington DC was the Orange Ponchos. Now, I am not talking about some faded-out, light orange colored ponchos. I'm talking Florida Orange---really, neon orange!! They were so orange that you could spot them from a mile away—which was the point, after all!! And of course, as we walked all over our Capitol, the rain came down just in sprinkles; but it was enough of a rain to require the wearing of our ponchos!! To the mortification of both Michael and Shara, we donned those ponchos and went on our way---Michael not choosing to walk along side me anymore but now with his also-suffering and slow-walking sister. (Most parents will recognize why I chose the very bright colored ponchos; I remained ever mindful that someone could snatch either or both of our precious miracles anytime they wanted to, and we were, after all, in the BIG and 'SCARY' city of DC!! I believed that Neon Orange was somewhat of a deterrent to "snatchers".) Ed and I, in our own neon orange ponchos, giggled at the slump-shouldered backsides of our two foot-dragging kids as we walked up and down hills and steps and into parks---enjoying the sites of our wonderful Capitol. Fortunately, for Michael and Shara, it did not rain every day while we were in DC!

And speaking of the Washington DC trip, I am reminded that--- and would be remiss if-- I didn't mention the fact that this trip would be where Michael and his sister discovered the joys of room service and cable television!! We never had our cable connected at our Trailwood home in order to encourage our two kids to continue their love of playing outdoors---we did not want them to become mini couch potatoes! I believe our plan worked, too--at least until the advent of Michael's TRS80. Anyway, I can see Michael lying—-leisurely---in one of our hotel room's big Queen-size beds---his sister in the other bed---both transfixed by the cartoons and shows (Disney, Discover, Animal Planet, and The History Channel being their favorites) that cable television offered. When they both indicated that they were hungry for breakfast---or was it dinner after a long day's walk around DC?--Ed and I decided to treat them to room service---they would be able to remain relaxed in bed and continue to enjoy the cable shows. What a Pandora's Box we opened that day!

When the food arrived and was brought in to the room by the waiter---and Michael and Shara realized that they didn't even have to move off the bed to eat (let alone get up and get dressed!), they were both ecstatic! From that day on, the biggest treat by far—-while staying overnight in a hotel-- was being able to order room service! We discovered we, as parents, had to step it up a bit—so later, when we found ourselves at the very exclusive Lincoln Hotel in Tampa, we allowed the kids to order whatever they wanted from room service! Big surprise! They both ordered French fries and grilled-cheese sandwiches—always a favorite at the Yonkers' residence!

Since this DC hotel experience is on my mind right now, I'd like to quickly mention the hotel's unusual pool. It was located on the hotel's roof!! And even though it was really cold up there—this was a really tall hotel!!—and neither Ed nor I could stand to get into the truly icy waters of the beautiful pool, both Michael and Shara frolicked in it like it was a hot-tub!! When Michael finally got out of the freezing water, his lips were a nice shade of periwinkle blue tending toward violet, and he was shaking and shivering like the proverbial leaf! I bear-hugged him into a towel--all the time he was insisting that he was NOT cold! Needless to say he did not get back into that pool again, and his sister got out shortly after he did, shaking all over herself! Neither of them asked to visit the pool a second time. But when we got home to West Palm Beach, they both were able to tell their Nana and Grandpa Godwin that they had actually swum in a pool on the roof of a very tall hotel in Washington DC!

24

There was a very interesting building—one of many interesting buildings we saw---in Washington DC. It was a building designed by a very famous architect named I. M. Pei, and it had the most incredible structural design as its walls came to a point rather than a squared corner. Michael was intrigued by unusual things---things that caught his artistic eye in ways different from ordinary things. While most of us were and are astounded and awed by Pei's vision—or by that upside-down house built in Orlando on International Drive—or by that most impressive castle in Germany—Neuschwanstein near Munich (We refer to this castle as "Michael's castle"); Michael was able to see immediately the whimsical in Pei's structure and in all the other unusual and wonderful things we have seen over the years. Spook Hill behind Bok Tower in Lake Wales really made him giggle—and then he began to figure out the mysteries of that anomaly---how could we travel uphill without using the gas pedal? He saw the raw beauty in these things, too, and he even captured the beauty in a most amazing re-drawing of his favorite German castle---a drawing that earned him a Blue Ribbon at an art show in Tequesta—when he was attending Jupiter High School. He went on to distinguish himself in the field of art by winning many artistic awards. Truly his output of art from elementary to middle school and through high school was outstanding. I have a vase that he made---I refer to it as the Colored Brick vase even though he never named this piece--which earned him praise and another Blue Ribbon at an art exhibition. It is as beautiful as any artistic vase I have ever seen. His early attempt at silk rubber stamping---a beautiful snake---is also a favorite of mine and resides on an end table in my living room.

When Michael was 4 years old, he wanted to enter an art contest sponsored by the Palm Beach Post Times newspaper. He competed against other children who were all older then he was. He won that contest because he finished the coloring with his own personal vision. He did things to the picture that nobody else would have thought to do. I had to really encourage him to complete the coloring so he could enter the contest. I wanted him to know that he could do anything---that he was very good at what he did---that others would also see how well accomplished he was; and I wanted him to realize the importance of committing oneself to something then seeing it through to the finish. Of course as so often happened where Michael was involved, I learned a valuable lesson, too---from him. He didn't really care if he won anything! He did things for his own pleasure of accomplishing something and didn't need the praise from others. Unfortunately, I wasn't as quick as my Michael---it took me years to learn this lesson while he was always living it!

25

I know I mentioned Michael's severe allergies as a reason we could not have a dog, but I didn't cover the half of it! He was almost always sick in the fall, and even though he always had a great costume, he rarely ---as a young boy—got to go trick-or-treating on Halloween. It broke my heart to see him standing each year—all dressed up in his costume—his jaunty pumpkin candy/treat holder held tightly in his hand-- his little legs crossed---staring out of our living-room front windows (windows built low to the ground—just perfect for a little boy to peek out of) waiting patiently for all the many trick-or-treaters who would make their way to our door. Even his two cousins, Dorrie and Barbie, would come knocking. Maybe this inability to celebrate Halloween as a little boy is the reason why---when Michael grew up—Halloween became a very favorite Holiday for him. He and his Laura have had some crazy, funny, wild costumes over the years!!

When Michael was little, he also suffered from asthma—part of the allergy syndrome for him. Our Pediatrician, Dr. Greene, said we needed to have allergy tests done on Michael to determine the extent of his problems. During the testing (two rounds), his entire little back was covered in needle pricks 2 or 3 times with small amounts of things like grass, dirt, dust, pollen, egg, peanut, etc—all put into his skin to see what reaction he might have---if any. We looked for big, red welts as this would reveal what he was allergic to—he reacted to all of the needle pricks! His back was covered in angry-looking welts. And when his asthma was really bad--- always late in the night—and he was so very scared because he felt like he wasn't able to breathe---I would sit with him in his bathroom with the hot water faucets all turned on high to create the steam which helped him to breathe easier. I needed to help him to stay calm as this was key to stopping his allergic reactions. We also had a gigantic, brown bottle of Quibron—the disgusting tasting medicine that the doctor prescribed for him in order to clear his lungs and/or bronchial tubes. I sat with him in my arms –on the toilet seat—and rocked him and sang to him---silly songs to get his mind off of his terrible wheezing, and I gave him a candy to take away the awful taste in his mouth—the taste caused by the medicine. When we built the Trailwood house, we did so with Michael's allergies in mind. There was NO carpeting on "his" side of the house and NO drapes (both are considered dust magnets!). We had black-out shades and Verticals on those windows. The living room, master bedroom, and the den had carpeting; and there were drapes only on the living room windows and the master bedroom windows. Years later we put some light weight, white, " girlie" curtains in Shara's room---kept them washed weekly---and these didn't seem to bother Michael's allergies. Thanks to Boomer Petti's (and Troy's) dad--Richie--who was in the decorating business and even did all the drapery measurements himself--we had top-of-the-line drapes installed; for 14 years we were able to keep them clean and in wonderful condition, and Michael's allergies were not affected. As Michael grew into a teen, his allergies became more manageable, and they seemed to be less of a problem for him. He did wheeze whenever he was sick, but his asthma attacks lessened considerably as he grew older.

We were both very happy to be able to throw away the crusty-topped big, brown Quibron bottle because he no longer needed to use it!

Many people like to refer to teenagers as "lazy, listening-impaired, semi-adults" who will revert back to their childish ways whenever it's convenient for them to do so. One late afternoon—when we were still living at Trailwood—Ed asked Michael to help him do a few things---things other than Michael's usual chores. Michael was in charge of keeping our backyard 40x20 foot pool clean and chemically balanced; also, he was to keep his own bedroom neat and tidy (which his room ALWAYS was because Michael was fastidious about his personal cleanliness!) When he was older, he also assisted his dad in the immediate fenced-in backyard area around our pool by holding a piece of plywood board to deflect the grass clippings Ed was mowing around the pool. The plywood helped to keep mown grass clippings out of the pool and made for easier cleanup. This last job Michael did grudgingly but with the knowledge that "his" pool wouldn't need as much cleaning care if he successfully kept the grass clippings out!!

On this particular late afternoon when Ed asked for Michael's help, he was trying to get the cars washed before dark, and he asked Michael to please help him get this done. After a whole lot of mumbling and foot dragging, Michael finally picked up a sponge and S-L-O-W-L-Y began to wash the side of the little, white Toyota station wagon---the car he would be driving when he earned his FL Driver's License. I guess if he had known the Toyota would soon be his car to drive, he would have gladly helped keep it clean and probably would have been on our cases to clean it more often! Anyway, they finally finished washing the cars, and Ed began to clean up. Michael's attitude had not changed much--he was still mumbling and obviously put out because he had been roped into doing yet another chore! Ed was dipping and wringing out his own sponge in the bucket he had filled with clean water and was placing the sponge, rags, and towels out to dry on the concrete driveway when Michael---holding his own sopping wet, soapy, dripping sponge in his hand and away from his body----turned and looked at his dad and asked in a most surly tone, "How do I clean this sponge?" Ed had really had enough of Michael's uncooperativeness and just looked up at Michael from his bent position, placing his wrung-out sponge on the ground, and with great but forceful patience, answered him, "JUST SUCK ON IT!" After Michael wiped the surprised expression off of his face---for his dad rarely ever lost his temper or patience with his kids---and he and his dad began to laugh "up-riotously!" I happened to come out to the opened garage at the time and asked what was so funny, beginning to giggle myself. Neither Michael nor his dad could stop laughing long enough to tell me. It was a while before I heard the complete story of "suck on it!"

Michael loved receiving and reading all the children's magazines we subscribed to when he was growing up. He particularly liked Enter Magazine, Sesame Street Magazine, and any and all of the Scholastic publications. When he was about 9 or 10, he read a very interesting story about a man who lived in Tasmania and who built very intricate, large ships out of matchsticks or toothpicks—I forget which. As usual, Michael had a million questions about this man and his hobby, and the article, itself---questions which ranged from, "Where is Tasmania?"; "How do you get there?"; "What's the weather like there?"; "How did he learn to do that?"; "How much time does it take to build his ships?" to "How does he keep track of how many sticks he uses for each ship?" Since he really did have numerous questions which I certainly couldn't answer, I suggested that he write a letter to the gentleman and ask him for answers to his questions. Michael responded, "He will never write to me because he doesn't even know me!" After much doubtful rumblings, he settled down to write a very lengthy letter to the man featured in an article in his favorite magazine! We went to the Post Office to mail his letter, and then typical of a 9/10 year old, he promptly forgot about his letter and the interesting man in Tasmania.

Not long after we mailed his letter, a letter arrived in our mailbox for Michael from Tasmania. That kind man had answered all of Michael's questions and had even included a few of his own questions for Michael. He wanted to know, "Where is Jupiter?"; "Do you like to go on boats on the water?"; "Do you have any hobbies?"; and "Do you make things?" The two of them wrote to each other, answering every question asked. They discovered that they had many interests in common. They continued their correspondence until Michael stopped receiving letters. We read in a future issue of the magazine that the kind old man who had built beautiful ships from sticks had passed away. Michael chose to honor this man's memory by taking Popsicle sticks and making a very lovely box for us; we still have and use the box today.

The idea of Popsicle sticks triggers another poignant memory of young Michael. He really loved eating Popsicles when he was a little guy---especially in the hot days of summer---but he would refuse to take them in his hands. Eventually, I realized that he had a real aversion to the sticky mess the Popsicle made, dripping all over his hands, clothes, and shoes. While he would devour a cut-up Popsicle in a bowl, he would not touch one on a stick! One time when Curry Hinton was about 2 years old, her mom, Mary, had an emergency and needed me to babysit for a while. One of the quickly given instructions I received from Mary was that Curry loved Popsicles---but I should first put her in the bath tub—filled with water---BEFORE I gave her the Popscicle. That way she wouldn't get sticky and want to get wiped every few seconds---and her clothes and shoes would remain spotless and sticky-free!! I discovered this method of Popscicle delivery also worked for Michael!! We used it in the bath and in his little wading pool! We even expanded the idea to include large lollipops. Michael enjoyed many Popsicles and lollipops in the bath and his pool----and his summers were complete---as they should be for every child----summers full of lollipops and Popsicles!!!

29

From the time he was a baby, Michael always had music in his life every day. He went to sleep with music from his little radio every night, and he would hear me sing, whistle, play my guitar or my clarinet during the day. I hold a vivid memory of him in my heart and can still see him with his little mouth puckered---trying to force a whistle out-- with his serious, contemplative eyes staring at me. It took some time, but he finally mastered the art of whistling. (In fact he was so successful that, most times, we had to beg him to stop!) He loved to play records, too---it didn't matter if we played my records or his records. He loved to have music on in the house. We would dance and sing to all the records, either holding each others' hands or with me holding him tight in my arms.

He especially liked Kermit the Frog and the song he sang on Michael's Sesame Street 1 Original Cast Record album---*Bein Green*—in which Kermie talks about how hard it is to be different—to be green. His musical tastes also ran to Captain Kangaroo---his record labeled *Good Morning Captain-Captain Kangaroo Original Cast Music*—was a particular favorite, many of the songs subtly teaching children how to live successfully in this world of differences. Disney records were popular and so were the records that I had listened to in my youth. Michael even liked the old records that had belonged to his Nana, my mom, when she was a little girl. He liked to sing along to the songs *Michael Finnegan* and *There Was a Little Girl Who Had a Little Curl*.

Of course in his teens, Michael moved right in to Metallica and one of my earlier favorites, Molly Hatchet! He also listened to Pink Floyd, but I never confessed to him that this group was one of my favorite groups of all time!! I thrilled when I heard Chicago or Queen emanating from the radio speakers in his room. I enjoyed almost all the musical sounds that drifted from his room and permeated throughout our house. I couldn't let on to him that I actually found pleasure in listening to his kind of music because parents, after all, weren't supposed to embrace the music of their teenage sons! (It was different in my day. My mom absolutely loved to listen to Elvis Presley perform; my friends' parents thought that Elvis was disgusting, and they were forbidden to listen to such "trash." I thought my mom was so cool. I wish I would have been brave enough to confess to Michael how much I enjoyed his music!)

Anyway, it was inevitable that Michael's love of music would grow and blossom into a desire to play a musical instrument. This development excited me to no end as I had had so many positive experiences in junior high and high school as a member of my schools' bands---Conniston Junior High School Band and the Forest Hill High School Mighty Falcons Band. Michael wanted to play the drums—just like his Uncle Bob (Godwin) did and still does. Bob was an outstanding drummer and he still performs to this day! Unfortunately for Michael, band "rules" had been established at Jupiter Middle School, and the Band Director said that he didn't need any more drummers---but he sure could use a trombone player. While I realized that

Michael had the "lips" for this instrument, I also knew that he was devastated at this news because he had no interest in playing the trombone. I went to the director and asked if he could please reevaluate his needs---at least listen to Michael play. I really wanted Michael to be a part of the whole band experience. Reluctantly, the director gave in and gave Michael an audition. Michael was exceptionally good for a young drummer and played well enough to make it into the band. The Band Director made it clear to me that he was not happy with what he saw as my "interference." I tried to stay in the background, volunteering where and when I was needed, but I never felt comfortable with that director again. The bottom line was that Michael was thrilled to be playing the drums in the band. We even bought Michael his own drum set so that he could practice at home. He already had a practice pad, but that fell out of favor after he got his drum set. Because we lived in the country and lived acres away from our neighbors, he could just wail away on those drums and cymbals all he liked without fear of disturbing the neighbors! Nobody ever complained or gave any indication that his playing/practicing annoyed or bothered them in any way.

The "rules" for band members extended into Jupiter High School, and when Michael "graduated" from Jupiter Middle School and went to the band try-outs at Jupiter High, he was, again, sorely disappointed. He was told by the High School Band Director that if he was allowed to join the Warrior Band, he would only be playing the cymbals. I had explained to Michael about the band practice called the "challenge." He asked the director if he would ever be able to improve enough to be able to challenge for a position as drummer. He was told he would not. So, Michael made the decision not to join the high school band. It saddened me that he never was able to have that high school band experience.

Ed and I were not unlike any other parents. We thought we were raising a brilliant genius of a boy! And, of course, I was always sharing stories that reflected Michael's latest clever antic. Fortunately for me, most of my cohorts also had clever geniuses at home, too---be they genius children or pets!! One day a guidance counselor friend offered to test Michael to try to pin-point his IQ. Since he was used to coming to Palm Beach Gardens High with me during pre-school and post-school---and since he knew the person who would be testing him, both Michael and I decided this testing would be something he would be able to do.

There was some shock felt by Ed and me when we were told after all the testing and "figuring" that Michael's IQ hovered somewhere around 155! We giggled; he REALLY was a genius!! Because he was so young (just 4 years old or so) when we had him tested, it was very difficult to get a more accurate number for his IQ. Years later, he would be tested for the public school Gifted Programs---the first time the test was administered at Allamanda Elementary School in Palm Beach Gardens—and we were told that his IQ was, indeed, in the 160's. He was tested once more, but by then, we weren't interested in the numbers so much as the quality of the education he was receiving. For the most part, his years of schooling in Palm Beach county Public schools were most satisfying---both to Michael and to us.

Michael used his "gifts" to accomplish many wonderful things in his life---both in school and later as a successful entrepreneur and businessman. I don't think he was always totally comfortable with all the "gifts" he had, but he certainly made the most of them! And the results of his making the most of these "gifts" is a blessing that has been shared with everyone he has ever known.

While I have indicated that Christmas was always an exciting holiday for Michael and the rest of us, and all holidays and celebrations were embraced with bubbling wonder by Michael, it was always a daunting challenge to make his birthday even more special for him. Michael's birthday fell on January 12th, which is very close to December 25th!! Because Christmas was such an important and highly anticipated holiday, we lamented the fact that we only had a mere 18 days in which to build on the excitement before we celebrated his special day!

Sometime during the 5th grade we think---it might have been earlier—while Michael was at Allamanda Elementary, we began to realize that Michael was becoming a computer lover (really a geek—but that word had not been heard of in 1982.) We knew he was going to want---no, need---a computer of his own---sooner rather than later! His school offered him the time and equipment to practice and hone his computer skills, but he would need to have one to work on at home. In Ed's job at the time, Ed was putting together the insides (the "guts") of the IBM computers; this knowledge just served to inflame Michael's desire even more---to have a computer at home. Eventually, we would have the used parts of one of those IBM computers, (and thus a PC for our family's use at home); but what we needed to do first was to find something for our son.

Ed and I found ourselves one day at Radio Shack in the Twin City Mall in Lake Park just off Northlake Blvd. We stood in that store knowing little to nothing about computers, and the one person who could help us with our choices was the one person we couldn't ask---Michael! This was to be a major surprise for him on his birthday. We were "sold" by the (maybe?) confident salesman on the TRS80 and all the "extras" that came with it. Michael had been preparing for the day when he would have a computer of his own by taking lessons after school---at least once a week. His teacher was Mark Craddock, the very competent son of one of Michael's teachers at Allamanda and a beloved student whom I taught at Palm Beach Gardens High.

Somehow we were able to keep the very exciting secret of the TRS80 from Michael. I remember the day when his birthday came that year; he awoke to find little notes-- which contained clues about his gift-- all over the house and even outside. It was a glorious treasure hunt, and we were as excited as Michael was as he read and deciphered each clue. Shara, Ed and I giggled our way all through the "hunt," and we enjoyed the excitement that was building in our son. By the time he found his gift in the very large closet off our bedroom, Michael was beside himself with joy. The large box proclaimed that a TRS80 resided within! He began doing flips and jumping all over and around the box. We referred to our closet---affectionately--as the "nursery" because of its large size; and on this day, that was a very good thing!! Michael needed all that room to vent all of his excitement. He finally settled down to open all of the boxes, first fixing us with his mile-wide smile!!

32

Before we moved to Trailwood in 1981, the July 4th Holiday was one that found us traveling, as a family, to the nearest fireworks show we could find. When we lived at the Lake Park Apartments, the 3 of us, dad, me and Michael, would just walk down to the Intracoastal Waterway to watch the spectacular show; but when we moved to the Green House on Palm Road in West Palm Beach, we had to get in the car and travel pretty far to see anything. Even when we moved to the rental house in Jupiter (fondly referred to as the Yellow House), we still had to get in the car to go see the fireworks show. Michael (and, later, Shara) always was enthralled by the beautiful displays of lights and designs that appeared in the darkening sky--- and he was probably excited by all the noise, too!! When we moved "way out" west of town to Trailwood, getting into the car and traveling a good long distance to see and hear a fireworks show no longer was seen as an exciting undertaking---at least not like it once had been. We began to bemoan the fact that there would be huge crowds consisting of grumpy adults and screaming children; it would take "forever" to find a parking spot—usually a very long hike from where the fireworks display would be; it was always so very hot the day of the display; and the mosquitoes would bite us without mercy!! And, there were fewer and fewer sites to choose from as many towns and groups who previously sponsored these events were no longer willing to bear the expense and liability of putting on the shows. But Michael couldn't stand the idea of not having fireworks on the 4th of July. He and his dad decided that they would put on a show for our family (and anyone who wanted to join us!) So, Michael devised a clever launching pipe, with the help of his dad, and we were ready for the first "Show." We had purchased a number of different kinds of fireworks at a rather large tent that had suddenly appeared one day in town on an empty lot. I knew nothing about these things, but Ed and Michael talked to each other as if they had been born setting off fireworks! We were ready for our July 4th celebration, and we would have our fireworks at home. The idea was that the rockets, spirals, rings, palms, chrysanthemums etc. would be launched from our front yard and would "explode" over the lake which was across the street from our house. Having our fireworks go off over water meant that we would be protecting the land from fires or other mishaps. We had our traditional cookout of hamburgers and hotdogs, cleaned up the kitchen and got ready for the evening's show. Shara and I placed our folding lawn chairs out front on the concrete driveway. And after wrapping Shara in a huge comforter to help ward off any mosquito attacks (Shara was the sweetest one of all of us and thus the one who was always targeted the most by these pesky, hurtful insects!), we sat down to watch the show. My recollection is that Michael and Ed's shows were 100 times better than any others we had seen---or have since seen! We laughed loudly at the "duds" and "oohed" and "ahhed" over the successes—and there seemed to be an inordinate amount of "duds" which had us giggling even more! As a family, we made our own July 4th shows, and they were the best because Michael wouldn't have it any other way!!

When Michael was 11 or 12 years old, we joined a Reform Temple that was forming here in Jupiter. Imagine our delight and awed surprise when we first walked into the old Jupiter High School meeting room (just off the library where those meetings were held on Friday nights) and discovered the Rabbi for this new temple was none other than Rabbi Friedman, the same Rabbi who had Bar Mitzvahed Ed's and my oldest nephew, Erik Covitz, in his temple in Massachusetts!!! It's a small world, no? The Rabbi and his wife had decided to retire to Florida, but they quickly found that retirement wasn't for them. They decided to "take on" this newly forming reform Temple and help build it into a permanent one here in Jupiter. Ed and I soon discovered that they were both wonderful working with children. The Rabbi's wife had developed a puppet show with which she was able to teach the children many valuable lessons, and the Rabbi had camaraderie with the pre-teens, especially with those who were full of questions. And Michael certainly fit that description!!

Unfortunately, the year Michael began studying for his Bar Mitzvah, the Temple congregants began exhibiting some in-fighting and some "political" strife. We found ourselves on the "losing" side of all this strife as we supported the Rabbi. The "problem" stemmed from the fact that some congregants thought the rabbi was "over-reacting." He had the "audacity" to ask these congregants to please control their young children's behavior during the Friday night services---and that behavior was certainly out of control! The children were allowed to run up and down the aisle, yelling and screaming, throughout the services. He suggested that the Saturday morning services might be better suited to the little ones, especially since there were classes for the children on Saturday mornings. Boy, did that suggestion bring anger and wrath down upon our Temple! The offended congregants moved quickly to put the Rabbi in his place.

The last time we ever attended services, as a family, at the temple, we had to sit and listen to the complaints being touted about the Rabbi---many from the young parents who couldn't or wouldn't control the bad behavior of their own children; and they had rallied supporters from the rest of the congregation—most notably the members of one of the Temple's founding families. Michael leaned over to me and quietly asked if he could speak. Before this meeting, I knew there was to be a discussion, and I had encouraged both Michael and Shara to speak about their feelings if they wanted to speak. Michael stood up after being recognized, and he made his case for the Rabbi. He said that Rabbi Friedman was an excellent teacher, that he loved coming to temple for his special lessons with the Rabbi, and that he had learned a whole lot from the Rabbi. In his frustration, Michael also said that I had told him once that "there was enough stress and trouble in everyday life---we should be able to come to Temple to find some peace!" Michael also told the congregation that the rabbi's wife was really good at teaching the kids, too, because his sister was learning so much, too. He told them that he looked forward to his own Bar Mitzvah ceremony, but he would not do it at this Temple if he couldn't stand next to Rabbi Friedman when he read from the Torah.

Of course the Temple replaced Rabbi Friedman, using the excuse that he was just "too old" for such a young and growing Temple. But Michael knew the truth, and he did not get Bar Mitzvahed at that Temple---even though Rabbi Friedman tried very hard to talk us –and Michael--into staying. So, where did Michael get Bar Mitzvahed? Why, in our home at Trailwood---and it was a service much like the ones Jews must have had during the war years. His own father over-saw the ceremony, and we used a miniature Torah that Michael had been given and had encased in a homemade ark. He read from his section of the Torah using a magnifying glass as the writing in the miniature Torah was very small. Rona Craddock, his teacher from Allamanda, was invited to attend the service, and she promptly picked up our movie camera and filmed the entire event for us! We served traditional Jewish foods—yummy goodies which we had ordered from the Too-Jay's Deli in Loehman's Plaza in Palm Beach Gardens. Many of Michael's closest friends were invited to attend this, his most special day---the day he would become a man by Jewish law. But I believe Michael became a man sooner than on this date---January 12, 1986. He did so in my eyes when he stood in the Temple and defended the Rabbi, a man who had obviously taught Michael so well!

34

One time when Michael was just a little guy, Janie (Morse) Donlon and I (I forget who else went to visit with us) went to visit our sorority sister, Judy Saurino, and her kids. Her Jimmy was about Michael's age and was her precious, handsome, dark-haired boy---special too---because he fought so hard to live. He had been born with medical problems—not the least of which was Cerebral Palsy. Judy and her family lived out west of North Boca Raton on a farm which was part of the Saurino Family Compound. They had some interesting animals living on the Compound, especially beautiful horses. After visiting with Jimmy and after Judy was done feeding him, we waited until his mom had put Jimmy down for his afternoon nap then prepared to go outside.

Judy joined us and we all went outside to see all the wonderful sights on that lovely piece of land. We went over to the place where the horses were kept. I was a little nervous---I always had had a fear of large animals. Also, Michael was with me, and that added another layer of fear for me. But I was determined and careful not to let my fear transfer to Michael as I did not want him to feel the same paralyzing fear I had felt most of my life. We walked down the center of the stables and "met" and "spoke" to the horses in their individual stalls. And when we reached the last stall, there stood the biggest, most beautiful horse I had ever seen! He was GIGANTIC!! Judy explained that he was at least 17 hands tall---a very large horse, indeed! (Horses who stand 17 hands are about 68 inches—5 feet 6 inches tall--, 172.72 cm, or 1.7272 meters and they weigh somewhere around 500 to 600 kilograms, or 1,100 to 1,300 pounds! The largest horse in recorded history was probably a Shire horse named Mammouth—born in 1848. He stood 21.2 hands high and his peak weight was about 1,500 kilograms, which equals 3,300 pounds!)

Anyway, I was a little "shy" shall we say to get very close to this humongous horse. But Michael was a different story—he didn't seem to notice anything odd or scary about the animal that HAD to resemble a skyscraper to a little guy like him!! Obviously size did not intimidate Michael because he reached out his little hand to this huge beast. My breath stopped in my throat; I watched—immobilized--as my son and this horse became acquainted. Could a horse--THAT size-- even SEE Michael's little hand reaching out and stroking the quivering leg? Judy picked Michael up, I gulped and let out a breath, and Michael reached out and connected with that beautiful animal's nose. The look on Michael's face I was to see only a very few times in his life---it was like he was in a different world—like he was viewing a paradise nobody else had ever seen before---a wonderfully mesmerizing place---and his face reflected such an old look of peace, incongruous on a face that young. Judy asked if it would be okay if Michael sat on that horse and went for a little ride. Now, you know I must have had great faith in Judy because after a long pause, I finally did say a very quietly weak "yes" in answer to her question. And Up

Michael went, sitting proudly up on that horse with Judy and someone else walking alongside them as horse and rider rode together around the yard!

Michael loved every minute he spent being with that horse. Though I still have a healthy regard and respect for large animals (like horses)---especially ones I don't know—I am pleased to say that with the advent of my medication for depression in 2002, I do not have the overwhelming, unbridled fear of them that I suffered in the past. And Michael NEVER developed a fear of animals—large or small!!

35

You know, not everything that turns out great in life begins that way! When Michael was 4 years old, he still wasn't able to swim. I was very concerned about this---as was his dad---because I felt he had to have this skill in order to survive—especially because of all the water we are surrounded by here in Florida. Michael would 'fight" me every time I brought up the idea that we should sign him up for swim lessons. We would go to Nana Godwin's house and swim in the Olympic-sized pool that was just a short walk from her Cresthaven Condo. I would give both Michael and Shara "lessons" before we played in the pool. Shara loved all of it; she would go under water and come up laughing while Michael was careful not to get his face wet!

In the summer—or late spring—of 1977, I signed both Michael and Shara up for lessons at the YWCA located in downtown West Palm Beach. My good friend, Cathy Harvey---who had told me about this program-- brought both of her kids for lessons, too. She and Chuck lived in Horseshoe Acres and had a pool in their backyard; she wanted her son, Michael, and her daughter, Beth, to be able to swim so she wouldn't have to worry about "accidents" happening. Our Michael was not too thrilled to learn that we had arranged swim lessons for him! In fact he tried every ploy he could think of to get out of the lessons. He complained of a terrible stomach-ache, a cough (fake though it was), and my favorite—his leg was too tired—he would come out to me dragging one leg behind him! But there was no choice in this matter as we were determined to get him swimming before his next visit to Nana's pool that summer!

Rusty was a very competent, no-nonsense safety swimming instructor. She took NO guff---either from parents or crying children! I was a witness one time when she "ordered" over-protective parents to leave the pool deck area while she was instructing their children. Those same children would be screaming for their mommies or daddies each time they came up for air! I don't know who elicited the most empathy from on-lookers---the panicked parents or the manipulative kids!?! But the bottom line was that those same kids learned how to stay safe in the water, either by floating on their backs and/or by kicking to the side of the pool on their tummies!! Rusty never had to send me out as I never fell for Michael's lusty cries each time he surfaced to catch some more air during his lesson. I was able to see the bigger picture---I would be the mother of a 4 year old who could finally keep himself from drowning!! I will admit that it is not easy to watch as your child begs you to help him-- and when you don't rush to his rescue, he looks at you as if you have turned into Wonder Woman's (his favorite Super Hero!) worst foe!! Of course Shara, age 2, would be smiling and giggling each time she came to the surface for air! She loved the water, took to it like a mermaid, and learned how to flip over and float on her back with no assistance; and she also could paddle herself to the side of the pool. She learned to do all of these valuable skills before her older brother did! But learn them he did----fighting Rusty and his parents all the way!!

It does seem a bit ironic that Michael was to become such a fabulous, winning swimmer in his teens; he even kept his swimming skills honed throughout his adulthood. Every opportunity that arose that allowed him to get in the water throughout his young life---after age 4---was seized upon with great joy and pleasure. Remember---he and Shara were my dare-devils when it came to all of those water parks that our family visited over the years!!

36

Michael showed an interest, early on, in the martial arts. Years later---in 1996 I think---he would meet his Laura at Florida Atlantic University during a Cuong Nhu class. This oriental martial art was developed by Dr. Ngo Dong in Vietnam, and it blends many different elements from other forms of defense—both hard and soft styles, which is how it got its name: "cuong" which means "hard" and "nhu" which means soft in Vietnamese. Both Michael and Laura had signed up to take the same class and both did very well in the lessons. But even when Michael was a little boy---maybe 8 or 9---he had a real interest in the martial arts and decided he wanted to take some lessons and learn to defend himself with honor. So, we looked around for classes. This was at a time before Jupiter even had a Community Center, let alone classes in different sports, talents, or skills of this type. Anyway, we found ourselves meeting with a fellow who was giving class instruction to anyone who wanted to learn martial arts; and he was offering the classes at the "house" located on the north side of the Jupiter Inlet---right next door to the beautiful Jupiter Lighthouse. The classes were held around 6:00 or 6:30 in the evening. One stipulation for signing up for these classes came as a surprise the first night Michael showed up for class.

I remember driving Michael to his very first lesson. He was really excited to be taking his first lesson in martial arts. I think Karate or Taekwondo was what was taught. Karate is a Japanese martial art that was developed in the Ryukyu Islands, which is now known as Okinawa, Japan; in this "striking" art, one uses fighting methods called "te", which literally translates as "hand." To defeat an opponent—feet, knees, elbows, and hands are all used in this form. Taekwondo is a South Korean martial art form and like Cuong Nhu it also derives its meaning from its name: "Tae" means to "strike or break with foot"; and "kwon" means to "strike or break with fist"; and "do" means "way" or "method" or "art." Literally, this art form means the way of kicking and punching, and it is still used today to train soldiers in South Korea. Anyway, we got to the place where the lessons were held, and immediately we were led into a small, cramped air-conditioned room and were made to sit through a rather boring, older taped presentation about self defense in general and some basic rules that applied to all defense courses in particular. I remember being very grateful for the air-conditioning as it was July, and the heat --outside the room was awful--even in the evening!! As Michael and I vacated the little room when the tape was finished, we found ourselves entering a very hot and humid room. This was the room where his classes would take place! Surprise!! Because of Michael's young age, the teacher said that a parent also had to sign up to take the course with the child! Of course I loved my son, so I agreed to sign up to take the course!! (Did I mention I was the only female/mom in the group? I was also the most "challenged" person in the room—obviously lacking in certain skills that seemed to be innate in my male counterparts, kids and adults alike.)

But I hung in there. The two of us were sweating our buns off, and, worse, we were being eaten alive by huge mosquitoes---but we were learning the "moves."

I could not wait to get home to get a cool shower and some salve to put on all my "itches." Surprisingly, Michael did not have to be coaxed at all to get his shower and get ready for bed that night. I think he even beat me to the bathroom for a shower. Michael was a "night" person from a very young age and did everything he could think of to prolong the time he could stay up before it became a more intense battle of the wills—Michael's will against whichever parent was in charge!

We went to the next lesson, got eaten alive, sweated profusely, and went home to glorious showers. On the way to our third lesson, I was silently dreaming of a time when Michael and I would be showing off our expertise in this martial art form at a competition which we would both win when I realized that Michael had spoken to me. I blinked back to the interior of our car and saw Michael looking up at me from the passenger seat, a serious look in his eyes, and he asked, "Mom, do you think we need to take any more classes or have we learned enough karate/taekwondo?" I studied his very serious, earnest little face and said, "I think we're better at it than anyone else I know!" So we, by mutual agreement, skipped the class (and all the rest of the classes) and went and got a Carvel ice cream cone!!

While I have always believed that if you commit to doing something, you should follow through on that commitment—even taught this idea to my children—in order to build character---I obviously failed to practice this belief when it came to our defense lessons. But there were extenuating circumstances. I learned that sometimes it's wiser to follow your son's lead!! Doing so will sometimes lead to less sweating and a whole "lot" of less itching!!

37

(This entry was written in August of 2009—after I spent a few days recuperating from a virus, which I had caught when I took care of a sick Viktor so his mom wouldn't miss any more work. All I can say is no baby deserves to have **this v**irus!) And this episode reminds me about Michael and his history of illnesses. Michael really didn't seem to get sick as often as his friends. Of course his allergies really got him down and made the fall a rather uncomfortable season, but he really never seemed to get as sick as often as his sister would; and she would run a 105° temperature and scare her parents to no end! As a young boy and into his teens, he was rarely ill, but when he was, it was asthma that put him down.

I think Michael took very good care of himself because he always ate in a healthy way---even if he did avoid some vegetables—and loved to be outdoors either playing or participating in sports activities. Perhaps these activities helped to boost his immune system? Many of these activities were of Michael's own making! His skateboarding competitions set in our front driveway and neighborhood spontaneous baseball games are examples of this creativity. He loved to swim, and since we had a pool at our Trailwood home, that 20'x40' pool allowed us to really swim and to play wonderful made-up games; Michael and Shara were in the pool nine months out of the year!

I always marveled at his "perfect" build; to me he looked like he was meant to be an athlete. Of course I was just a little prejudice—being his mom and all---but I thought Michael was at first a precious little baby boy and then a cute little boy, then a good-looking young man, and finally, a knock-out, handsome man!! Perhaps there are others who would agree with my assessment of our son! And if there are those who would disagree—why, they are of no consequence to me! But I do have to say that Viktor's attributes are even more aesthetically pleasing than his father's were! He eats so much better than his dad did—loving vegetables like they were ambrosia of the gods. He is, of course, very cute—100 times cuter than his dad was---has the same perfect little build, is probably smarter (which is scary!), and is every bit equally as "busy" as his dad ever was at this age! Unfortunately, he seems to have developed the asthmatic problems his dad had, but he is better equipped to handle them and doesn't get quite as ill as his dad did.

Just because I say he wasn't often sick doesn't mean we didn't have just a few scares along the way! When Michael was about 2 ½ or so, he was playing in the house—being a wild monkey---and he was running away from his sister who was barely crawling and trying hard to keep up with her fast-as-lightning brother. He was so quick, but even though he easily escaped from her, he left her laughing and giggling at his antics, and this left her with no energy to even try to keep up with him. This pattern was to follow them into adulthood---her laughing at him and him escaping just out of her reach. On one particular day I was in the kitchen of the Green house trying to decide what to do for supper when the giggles and happy screams emanating from the living room were suddenly and abruptly stopped. An instant later there followed one awful, heart-stopping scream, then silence followed quickly by sobs. I rounded the breakfast bar not even aware that I had crashed my side into the hard wood to find Michael sitting on the living room rug next to the partial divider wall which separated the living room from the family room/dining room. Our Green house was not that large so this motion took all of two seconds. There he sat with a stunned look on his face—eyes truly as big as saucers—paler then the white paper towel I held in my hand. He was now quietly whimpering—such a sad sound brought cold fear into my stomach. He was holding his forehead with his shaky little hand. I bent and carefully removed his hand and saw a very deep cut running vertical over his left eye—but not reaching into his hairline. I knew it was a serious cut and would need medical attention. I carefully lifted him on to my hip. As I talked calmly to him—even though my insides were churning and my eyes begged to cry—he calmed down almost eerily so. I don't recall that he bled a lot from his wound, but he must have done so as there was much evidence of it on him and the floor. The cut was so deep, I could see bone. I quickly placed the wet paper towel I had grabbed—folded---to his forehead and told him to push hard on the paper towel. Michael did as I had directed him to do, but he was acting strangely--as if he were in a trance. I continued to talk calmly to him as I grabbed for his now crying sister and carried them both to the breakfast counter. I put Michael down in front of me—leaving my hand on his. I succeeded in calming Shara which proved easier once she was near her brother; then I reached for the wall phone and called our Pediatrician's office. Of course they advised me to bring him right in so the doctor could exam him. We did not live near the doctor's office—the Green house was located in the south-western part of Palm Beach County and Doctor Greene's office was located north of West Palm Beach off Olive Avenue, which was in the central-eastern part of the County. I was too scared to try to drive to the doctor's without having someone with me to keep watch over Michael as I feared he may have a concussion and would need to be kept awake. I quickly placed a call to Nana and Grandpa Godwin---they lived 5 or 6 minutes away from us in Emory at Cresthaven—and asked for their help to get Michael to the doctor's office. They were at our house in minutes and helped me get both Shara and Michael into the car and I began our frantic trip to the doctor's. Before we left, I had called Ed at his office and tried to calmly explain to him that Michael had cut his forehead and we were going to go to Dr. Greene's office; I could hear the fear and tears in his voice as he assured me that he would meet us at the doctor's. My dad held Michael in his lap; even though we had always followed the rules when it comes to child car safety, my dad was also afraid that Michael might have a concussion and wanted to have him close to keep him awake. Nana sat in the back seat next to Shara, making sure she was kept calm, too. How I drove to the doctor's that day I will never know—I have no recollection of the actual drive; as we approached the large medical building, I saw Ed pacing near the curb and in front of the doors—ready to take Michael in to the doctor's office without any more delay. My dad took over driving the blue Pontiac Grand Prix into the parking lot while I hopped out and went into the building with Michael and Ed. We were whisked right in to an exam room, and when Doctor Greene stepped into the room, he immediately assessed the situation; after looking first at Michael and his wound, he then glanced at us, the frantic parents, and he asked us to please step out of the room with his nurse. While Ed and I balked at the idea of leaving our traumatized son, we realized, in retrospect, that the doctor needed complete calm while he was tending to Michael's wound. We were anything but calm. The nurse ushered us out of the room while quickly explaining that Michael needed stitches and would be put in something called a "papoose." She left us in the hallway and returned to the examining room that held our precious son. We quietly walked to the outer waiting room to sit and wait for news of our son. We were to discover later that by using this device, the doctor was able to quickly stitch the wound closed. The "papoose" kept Michael from being able to struggle, yet it gave him the feeling of being held as it hugged his whole body. And it was most assuredly easier on Ed and me as we did not have to bear witness to our little boy being stitched up by the doctor!

As we sat and waited in the outer waiting room, I found myself finally being able to react to Michael's injury. Silent tears slowly rolled down my cheeks as I pictured Michael hurt and all alone—having to be brave while he got his stitches. Shara crawled into my lap and took my face in her hands, as if to say "don't cry, mommy." I was able to explain to Ed and my mom and dad just exactly what had happened at home—Michael's forehead had collided into the edge of the divider wall, and the hard hit nearly knocked him out. What seemed liked hours---but was more probably 15 to 20 minutes later—Michael came jauntily walking out with the smiling nurse, the inevitable lollipop in his hand. He wore a huge smile on his face which seemed out-of-place given his very puffy looking, moist eyes. He wore his "Badge of Courage" almost proudly as he showed the stitches to his Nana, Grandpa, and his Dad.

But I knew that this awful experience was not all forgotten—as we began walking toward the parking lot to get in the car for the drive home, Michael abruptly turned to me, let go of my hand, and put his arms up to me to be lifted and held---something he rarely did anymore—preferring to walk, run, skip, or jump his way to wherever we were headed! In that moment I felt that he was either comforting me or seeking the same for himself, and I gladly accepted his generous offer as I needed it every bit as much as he did!

Growing up, Michael always knew that Christmas Eve would be spent at Nana and Grandpa Godwin's home in Cresthaven in Lake Worth. Even when we moved to Jupiter, this tradition was always kept. For our entire family, it was one of the most anticipated evenings of the year because Nana would make all her food specialties, and the children would get to open a few of their Christmas presents---the ones from Nana and Grandpa and Uncle Bob and Aunt Nancy and their cousins, Dorrie and Barbie. The evening would commence as we sat down to a sumptuous feast; all of Nana's homemade salads of tuna fish, egg salad, and potato salad would be placed around the table. There would be pickles of all kinds—sweet, sour, and dill—and both kinds of olives---black and green pimento stuffed ones; there were mounds of thinly sliced tomatoes and crunchy green ice berg lettuce ripped into perfect sandwich-sized pieces; there was a full array of thinly sliced deli meats—every kind one could want; and there were three different kinds of bakery-fresh bread---whole wheat, rye, and pumpernickel. Accompanying all these delectable choices was a beautifully arranged cheese platter which contained a number of different types of cheese—all neatly cut and ready to be placed on a just-made sandwich! Condiments could be seen on the far ends of the oval-shaped table—to be passed to whomever requested them. Early on, potato chips were served because Michael didn't eat Nana's potato salad; but eventually, when Michael was a little older and perhaps wiser, the chips disappeared from the table completely—nobody was eating them!

We really had to learn to pace ourselves at this meal because we knew Nana would serve her usual desserts, and we needed to save room for them! Especially good were Nana's homemade cookies---Santa's Whiskers, Pecan Sandies, Melting Dreams, Praline cookies, and my own expertly baked chocolate chip Toll House Cookies. Truth be told, Michael always preferred the chocolate chip cookies---and fortunately both his sister and later his wife were experts at baking them for him! Even though Nana's pumpkin pie was a staple dessert at Thanksgiving, she began to bake one for this holiday as well because she knew it was Michael's all-time favorite dessert! Nana always made special coffee cakes for both my brother's family and for mine---either her Danish Ring cake or her Cherry Pecan Ring—or even a combination of these two cakes---and we were to take these cakes home and enjoy them on Christmas morning. We still have coffee cake on Christmas morning but have begun a different tradition as I make the cake from a recipe Joyce Hollobaugh, one of my beloved sorority sisters, has given to me—it's her Snapdoodle Christmas coffee cake recipe, and it is yummy!

After a very pleasant dinner, we cleared the table and cleaned up the kitchen while listening to all the taped Christmas/Holiday music playing in the background. Grandpa Godwin had painstakingly recorded and commentated on each selection culled from his massive record collection and put these selections on his tape machine. We still have those tapes of him announcing each song in his Yale-trained natural-sounding voice. I always had a favorite request, and dad was ready to play it—it became a favorite of Michael's, too—it was Spike Jones' *"All I Want for Christmas Is My Two Front Teeth."* Once this song was played—sometimes twice—we sat down to the presents.

After exchanging, opening, then "oohing" and "ahhing" over our presents, we gave "thank yous" all around. It was time to clean up again and begin getting ready for the drive home. It was a short trip for both Bob's and my family until Ed and I moved with the children to Jupiter—then it was a long drive home. Michael was always concerned--- when we finally said our last "good-byes"--about the lateness of the hour, and we often found ourselves racing Santa to get to our home—and fall asleep-- before Santa arrived. Michael and I would take turns peeking out the car windows as we sped north on the Turnpike; we searched the dark skies looking for any sign of the toy-covered sleigh. Not a few times, we saw the blinking red light that Michael was sure was Rudolph's red nose; and Michael pleaded for his dad to "hurry up and get us home!!" He was so afraid that Santa would skip our house if he wasn't in his bed where he belonged! Nothing we could say could convince him otherwise. And we were very fortunate because we always made it home in time to get to sleep before Santa could stop by and deliver his goodies!

40

As you may have guessed, it was never easy to stay ahead of Michael. He was constantly thinking and always trying to figure things out. Christmas Eve—<u>very</u> late at night—was an especially difficult challenge. Michael's excitement level had him awake until late into the night. He was just so worked up about what was about to happen in his house! Ed and I thought that he would stay in his bed for fear that Santa might see him up and out of bed; Michael was convinced that Santa would skip the houses of any children who did not obey the "stay home and stay in bed" rule. We didn't think he would take a chance that his house might be skipped over by Santa. However, we learned the hard way that Michael's adhering to the rule was not always the case. This one night we had waited until we were sure that he was sleeping before we got up, tiredly, to assemble and put out the many toys for under the tree. Today's parents have to deal with toys that are practically molded and sealed to their packaging (Home Depot has the perfect scissors for opening these pesky packages!), but the toys sold during Michael's childhood only required a great deal of physical labor on the parent's (dad) part in order for the toy to even resemble a toy!! Anyway, each year—as the children aged—it seemed that we were having to stay up later and later trying to get around Michael's great curiosity and what we came to believe was the toy-makers' revenge on unsuspecting parents—all because we parents were not buying enough toys to suit their bottom line-profit!

Michael had "caught" us a couple of Christmas Eves putting together toys, but his dad and I were always able to distract him and get him back to his bed before we destroyed his magical belief. But toward the end of one particularly rather long night, Michael came silently (and I think stealthily) down the long hallway and into the living room (our "workshop" area); he moved quietly on the proverbial "little cat's feet" just like Sandburg's "Fog!" Ed had exhausted himself trying to put together some stubbornly sadistic, difficult toy and was struggling with where to put the "extra" parts he held in his hands. I confess I was dozing on the couch. I came out of my sleepy slumber when I heard a very loud gasp—I sat up staring at our little boy who was gaping at and taking in the room with all its toys and wrapped presents under the Christmas tree and outlined by the blinking of the multi-colored lights from the tree. Thank goodness Ed was still thinking—and pretty quickly considering the lateness of the hour. He turned to Michael and said, "Can you believe that Santa did it again? He left these toys and forgot to put them all together!" Michael declared that that was okay—he and Ed could finish the job in the morning! With that, we all went back to bed—for about 2 ½ hours more sleep—Ed and I hoping that the next few years would still hold the magic for Michael. And they did!

In typical Michael fashion, as we drove home one Christmas Eve from Nana's and Grandpa's, Michael reminded us that he had fix-it tools now, and if Santa forgot to put all the toys together---we should just wake him up so he could help his dad put everything together!!! In fact, from that day on, Ed left the more difficult toys to put together with Michael's help on Christmas Morning.

41

Michael and his Laura really did have a fairy-tale wedding! Ed and I were so happy when Michael decided to ask Laura to marry him; we were taken with Laura from the first time we met her. We both walked on egg-shells over the next eight or so years wondering "when" or "if" and hoping that Michael would decide to ask her to marry him! Imagine our pure delight when he called and told us that he had bought a ring and was going to ask her! We were thrilled; for as much as we had come to love Laura, we found that her whole family was a perfect "fit," too! Michael did not have to be reminded that he needed to ask "Bear" (Laura's formidable dad) for Laura's hand in marriage. I guess George (Bear's formal name) must have said "yes" to Michael's request, but I am sure he gave Michael a thorough debriefing of his expectations as regarded his daughter because Laura was his "baby"—the youngest of his seven children--and because George has a wonderful sense of humor and is never afraid to use it!

Anyway, the wedding was planned with great precision and would take place on February 29, 2004 (Leap Year) in an ancient medieval Spanish monastery—which was originally built sometime between 1133 and 1144. The Cloisters were taken down stone by stone and shipped to the USA sometime in 1925. (The hay that each of the stones had been packed in had to be burned upon arrival because they discovered that the hay carried the hoof-and-mouth disease which had broken out in Segovia, Spain—the very town where William Randolph Hearst had purchased and had packed the Cloisters known as the Monastery of St. Bernard de Clairvaux. Unfortunately, the carefully numbered crates (to insure future, exact replication of the original monastery) were ripped into and broken open in haste in order to get at the hay [which might be carrying the dreaded disease] so that it could be burned. Because of the haphazard way the boxes were opened, it was impossible to put the stones back in their properly numbered boxes, but the packers did the best job they could.)

In 1952, after sitting in storage, the stones changed hands and were brought to Miami, eventually winding up in North Miami Beach, FL, and they were used in the building of an Episcopal church. (There is evidence on the grounds of the church which shows that not all of the stones were used to rebuild the church to replicate the original. This was a result of the hasty unpacking done in 1925.) This beautiful church's grounds were the magical venue in which Michael married his Laura. Of course the wedding party and most of the guests were dressed appropriately in medieval garb. And Ed had planned a huge surprise for his boy---he came dressed as a jester all in purple and black—tights, puffy pantaloons, silly 3-pointed jester hat, jester pointed-toe shoes, and a jester wand!! But the biggest surprise was the "performance" Ed would give to the gathering—and he did this all to show Michael how much he was loved and to foster the humor we treasured as a family.

At one point in the joyful evening, which was filled with sword fighting, fire-eating, and unbelievable tricks performed by a real magician, I came upon Michael who was just leaning on a half wall and hanging out with a few of his good buddies---sipping from his silver tankard filled with beer from a keg. I joined him, and we clinked tankards and took sips of our "ale" together. He asked me if I was happy as he stared intently into my eyes. I looked at him and said, "This is THE most magical fun night I have ever had in my whole life, and I am so very happy, especially for you and Laura!" He took a step toward me and with his mile-wide smile, he told me was glad. Then he gave me one of his much-coveted hugs. It had certainly been a most magical evening!!

42

Everyone who knew Michael would tell you he was a problem solver. From the time he was a little boy, he was always able to come up with marvelous ideas to solve most perplexing problems that someone might be experiencing. Here is just a very short list and quick explanation of some of the problems he was able to solve:

- While a student attending Allamanda Elementary School--and during a mock presidential campaign sometime before the 1984 Presidential election which pitted the incumbent Republican President Ronald Reagan and his running mate, George H. W. Bush, against the Democratic ticket of former Vice President Walter Mondale and his running mate, Geraldine Ferraro who was the first woman ever to be named a candidate representing a major American political party---Michael was able to design and help build a believable papier-mâché Statue of Liberty whose color exactly matched that of the real Lady Liberty and whose size was pretty impressive, too.
- After we moved into the Trailwood house, Michael saw that his dad had a real need for a place in which to conveniently store his tools. Michael devised a clever tool holder from a board that he sanded and stained; then he placed small white nails on the board that were strong enough to support his dad's tools. He attached a string from which to hang the tool holder, hammered a nail into the edge of the top wooden shelf that hung over Ed's workbench, and hung the tool holder so that Ed was easily able to reach for those tools, especially the ones that he used so often for fixing things around our house.
- Michael designed and built an intricate community for his and his dad's train set, which featured many home-made items on display; the project began when he found a plan for a train table in one of Ed's modern railroading magazines. He built the entire train table—the legs and the support beams for the plywood top---in the garage; then he placed a large piece of plywood on top of the sturdy under structure he had built--thus completing the train table. The table top even had a realistic looking Plexiglas covered lake—a lake that was formed even below the table top by cutting out a hole in the table top then connecting a light-weight plastic bowl to the bottom of the table top. The bowl had been covered inside with a thin layer of plaster which he painted to look like a lake and what looked like the bottom of a lake.
- Somehow Michael was able to keep our riding lawn mower in working order long after it should have bit the dust. Invariably, I would be in the middle of mowing our acre of property and the berm across the street that ran along the lake in Trailwood when the mower would just "die." It was so frustrating to have this happen---always in the summer when I was in the middle of trying to mow--and it happened more often than not!! Michael would come out of the house as I was pushing the mower up the driveway, come and take over by pushing the mower into the garage where he would

put it up on the ramps he had purchased as a gift for his dad. I would assist, but he was the one who figured out what the problem was and what needed to be done to fix it.
- Michael designed and built an extended wooden shelf which he attached to the top shelf of his Trailwood bedroom's built-in book shelves. He painted the extension the same color white that the existing shelves were painted. The shelf was just perfect for holding his small black and white 13 inch TV set!
- He helped to find and to fix up and to stain/paint some wooden spool tables that he and his dad surprised me with one Mother's Day. The little tables were placed in our Trailwood home's living-room and made splendid matching end tables on either side of our queen-sized sofa-bed; the tables perfectly matched my beloved telephone spool coffee table---the table where our family spent many wonderful Seders comfortably reclining on cushions on the floor while we ate from the dishes spread across the big table's top. The coffee table was made by brushing on multiple layers of Fiberglass—it took a great deal of time to make as each layer had to be given the proper amount of time to dry before the next layer could be applied. A good friend of "Aunt" Sara's and "Uncle" Richie's made it for us.
- When Michael was about 15, he was working toward becoming an Eagle Scout. One of the requirements for earning this rank is to select and complete an approved project. Michael decided that—for his project--he wanted to build a portable Crèche for the church in which his Boy Scout troop held their meetings. The Scout Leader was very pleased with this idea and so were the Pastor and church members. Michael designed a beautiful portable Crèche and brought the drawings in to make sure the project passed muster. The church had very limited storage space and its members were pleased to have something that would be easy to put up and take down and store! The finished project was truly a work of art and has served the church for many years.
- Like his Grandpa Godwin, Michael could also figure out and fix most problems that arose concerning cars. He usually got the cars in excellent running order by the time he finished! This skill became a real necessity after he bought a rather stubborn Pontiac Firebird. It needed just a whole lot of fixing!!
- One of the jobs Michael held before college but after he had moved out on his own was that of a foreman for an environmental abatement company. He devised a totally safe environmental plan for all the workers who helped to remove asbestos from the Helen Wilkes Hotel in downtown West Palm Beach. They were successful in this endeavor.
- He resolved and solved problems through his many school-based science projects, but he also assisted others by steering them to solutions.
- He solved the dilemma of providing us with an appropriate sized, inexpensive back patio for our current home. With HOA limitations, we needed to keep the project within certain rules. Michael and Laura surprised us by purchasing and installing 8 large marble

tiles off our back door pad while we were away. It was a wonderful surprise to come home to that new patio; we still enjoy our pretty, practical patio today, smiling when we think about the work Michael and Laura did just for us!

- When Michael visited Shara and Jason in their "new" Greenville, South Carolina home, he was asked to look at an area beneath their very impressive deck to see what they could do to make it look even better. He took one look then designed and "built" edging and steps which set off the already pretty area of stones and large and beautiful pieces of slate. The Lipscombs of Greenville still enjoy the fruits of Michael's labors despite the fact that Shara and Jason have long since replaced the upper decking with a totally different designed deck---a bigger, better and much more beautiful deck than the previous one was!
- When Ed and I moved into our present Villa, we wanted to replace the carpeting because the color of the carpeting was not to my liking even though it was in fine condition. We hated to waste this good carpet, but we had decided to lay beautiful, Italian 17" tile (which we had already ordered.) Michael came up to help us, and when he heard our dilemma about the carpeting, he began to tear out all the carpeting—assuring us that he had come up with a very practical use for the perfectly fine, left-over carpet. After pulling out the carpet, he took it to our garage and cut it to fit the entire area of our garage floor. To this day—nearly 15 years later---that carpet still covers our garage floor!
- When it became apparent to him that he did not have enough room for his lawn tools, machinery, and other yard-related things, he designed and built a perfect "little" mini-house in the far rear west corner of his "dream" house. When Ed and I first saw the finished work, I declared it a perfect little mother-in-law house!! Just add the plumbing, and we would be in business!! This structure was NOT your ordinary storage "shed."
- Michael was always able to resolve all of my computer problems and questions, sometimes by using his own unorthodox inventions. He was a master at figuring out how to get the computer and its programs to "work" as he needed them to work!
- As a fairly new business owner, Michael was able to develop the most user-friendly, innovative, complex, but easily understood systems and software and did all of the programming for one of our nation's largest trucking companies. He also did the same thing for another well-known company—General Electric—in GE's South American medical division.

This list just touches the tip of the iceberg of all the problems that have been successfully solved and resolved by our miracle boy! I have always tried to embrace the attitude that Michael (and Shara) could do whatever he (or she) set his (or her) mind(s) to do in life. I believe certain accomplishments in Michael's life were extraordinary examples of this same philosophy—if he "believed it, he could achieve it." And all our lives have been forever enriched because he believed in this philosophy, too!

We were lucky to be able to take a few trips to Greenville, South Carolina with Michael and also with Michael and Laura. We spent one Christmas at Shara and Jason's apartment off East North Street. It was really very cold that December, and Michael's asthma was giving him all sorts of breathing problems. But he "soldiered on," and we had such a memorable time. Ed and I had been assigned the "big" bed, and of course Frankie, our first Grand dog who was the smartest, most socially adept Basset Hound mix that ever hit a college campus, slept in the bed with us. (Years later, and a number of Grand dogs later, Jason re-trained Shara so that all dogs slept on their beautifully appointed dog beds-on the floor!) An air mattress and two couches made up the other sleeping areas. Despite the terrible cold (which I secretly loved), we had a wonderful, funny, game-playing time. Michael introduced us to "Mr. Hanky" that Christmas. Ed and I had never heard of let alone seen the TV show known as South Park---and we were in for a hilarious treat! We watched the show as best we could because tears were literally rolling down our cheeks----I laughed until my sides hurt. The Santa bit was truly genius and the best part of the show for me. We also played many games—both board ones and others like Charades---all day and into the night. And on Christmas, the four adult kids, Michael and Laura and Shara and Jason, really got into and played with their "toys"---toys that I had bought them as part of their Christmas presents to remind them that one never outgrows the need for the joy of having and playing with toys! Years later this "tradition" of giving Christmas toys each year to our adult children grew into a plot on my part to subtly and subliminally encourage the proliferation of Grandchildren! Hey, it worked!! We now have three wonderful Grandsons!!

Anyway, this particular Christmas Michael and Laura got the latest in what was to become their usual toys—Mr. and Mrs. Potato Head. (There have since been mermaids, pirates, key chain Potato Heads, Darth Vader Potato Head, Etch-a-Sketch Potato Heads---well, you get the idea.) Jason and Michael both received something that resembled a small, furry animal; these animal-like toys were battery operated and rolled around on the floor exhibiting all sorts of ridiculous maneuvers. These "pet" toys drove Frankie crazy, and I believe she either eventually ate or destroyed them both!

While still on our Greenville, South Carolina visit, we decided a ride to the North Carolina mountain area would be a welcome treat. We were on the inevitable quest to find me some snow; I yearned to see and touch it. Snow was an elusive weather phenomenon which I had yet to enjoy during any of our December visits to Greenville! The kids thought that my obsession to want to see and play in snow was a funny one. And this time we were rewarded---there was enough snow to throw a few snowballs at each other! The joke was that while it never snowed in Greenville, South Carolina while Ed and I were staying there, it certainly snowed AFTER we had left!! In fact there were a few times, including this time, when as we were leaving and I glanced out our car's back window, I could finally see a lovely, silently falling blanket of snow which was beginning to cover the entire view out the back window! (In January of 2009, it finally snowed in Greenville---enough to sled, have snowball fights, and build a tiny snowman---I thought it was just grand, and I noticed that Shara, Jason, Tyler, Trevor and Ed had just as much if not more fun playing in the snow than I had!)

During that ride in the North Carolina Mountains, we all laughed until we couldn't breathe. Frankie had something to do with our mirth and our inability to breathe!! Of course she came on the trip with us, sitting in the back seat with us for most of the trip. It seems that Frankie suffered from severe gas attacks----and we froze when we HAD to put down all our windows; but this was the only way we could keep breathing! We reverently referred to the gas emissions as Frankie's "broccoli farts!!" And it sure smelled awful! Lots of laughing always accompanied those trips to South Carolina, and many games were played and won---all with a great deal of laughter!

44

When Michael was just a little guy, we always marveled at how well behaved he always was. We could take him to restaurants and know that not only would he behave but he would wind up entertaining everyone within ear-shot of our table---from the wait staff to our fellow diners! He had a ready laugh and his mile-wide smile that just invited everyone around him to respond to him in positive ways. He reveled in positive feedback. But there were a few times—especially at home---when he would balk at something we were asking of him. And this non-cooperative behavior seemed out-of-character for him. The only way we could get him to "mind" at times like this was to resort to this veiled threat: "Do you want Mrs. Tucker to come and stay with you?" Uttering that one question, with the impact it held for Michael, could curtail his bad behavior immediately! With apologies to Mrs. Tucker, who was a wonderfully caring, competent childcare provider, here is an explanation as to how and why invoking her name brought Michael to his behavioral senses: Our friends, Cathy and Chuck Harvey, often went on vacations that required that they hire a reliable childcare provider to stay with their two precious children. At one point, they were very fortunate to find Mrs. Tucker—an elderly sweet, soft-spoken lady who was quite tall and who had rather large feet which were invariably ensconced in very sensible dark-colored work shoes. She was a lovely lady who was very competent—with a reputation that she could especially deal well with young, unruly children. From the moment the Harvey's found Mrs. Tucker, they used her services for all their baby-sitting needs; and there were a few nights when Ed and I also took advantage of Mrs. Tucker's expertise with childcare. We left Michael and Shara in her very adept care---beginning with having her "sit" several times with all four of the children at the Harvey's home. After engaging Mrs. Tucker's services—she would sit just for our kids in our home--we began to notice that our Michael acted a little bit shy---maybe even afraid—of Mrs. Tucker. It was after the third or fourth time she "sat" for the children that we realized he was truly and thoroughly afraid of her. We stopped using her services---not because she had done anything wrong but because we just didn't go out so often anymore. We quickly learned that we could use the threat of having Mrs. Tucker come over to babysit for Michael (and Shara) in order to keep Michael's behavior in check! I'm embarrassed to report that we successfully used this method of intimidation for a good two years to curb the behavior problems. Cruel of us? Perhaps. But we were just two desperate parents working from average IQs, and we were going up against Michael, after all!! He always seemed to be able to stay at least two steps ahead of us on most things; we HAD to use whatever method would work for us!!

Our family often laughed at the memory of the Mrs. Tucker threat. Even when Michael was a teenager---and displayed some unruly behavior—it still brought eventual smiles to our faces when we said to him, "Do you want Mrs. Tucker to…" And we NEVER had to finish that question because we were all broken up laughing at the memory that name invoked!

45

I can firmly and truthfully attest to the fact that whatever job Michael took on, that job would be done successfully. We did not push Michael into taking on the responsibility of a steady albeit part-time job when he was a teenager as we felt that his "job" during this time was to do well in school, help around the house with his assigned chores, participate in sports—both organized and at home—and get himself ready for the next step in his life---college. It was Michael who helped us to recognize that he needed to become a part of the work force as a step toward his independence. We watched him head off for his first job, working at a McDonald's in Jupiter. He wanted to earn his own spending money in order to put gas in the car when he used it, and to buy food when he was out, and to pay for all his fun activities. Of course he was a quick study and became a valuable employee in a very short time.

Even as Michael struggled through problems in his life, he continued to work. After leaving our home to live on his own and then graduating from high school, he became a foreman for an asbestos removal company and was lauded there for his close and successful attention to safety issues on the job. He worked in a Tee shirt- screen-printing and embroidery shop in Boca Raton for years—even while he was attending Florida Atlantic University--- and he was the employee whom they depended upon to keep their computer operated multi-head embroidering machines (computers whose precise work was very exacting and delicate) in good running order. He even took in some of their orders---one of which was from his mom and my Palm Beach Gardens High School Pep Club. The tee-shirt he designed was one of the best looking spirit shirts we ever wore---he also was able to do this job for a nominal price for our small club. When Ed and I had the pleasure of visiting Michael at this work site, we were very impressed. The building held a number of small rooms—one area was for the outer offices; there were a number of individual working rooms-- one of these working spaces was full of very complicated looking machinery (these were the embroidery machines) and there were hundreds of rows of all colors of threads and there were hundreds of designs that papered all of the available wall space-all the way up to the ceiling and running into adjoining rooms---these were machine-made designs and personally created designs that were used in past tee-shirt orders. There were other rooms that held machines that performed other jobs---like the inking on the tee shirts. While all of these things looked complicated to me and Ed they were easily identified by and run by Michael. Michael worked for several computer companies after he graduated from college with his Computer Science degree. The first person he worked for was Chuck Wheelus, who owned his own computer business---a business that dealt mostly with offering to other businesses space on his servers and that also offered some programming. Michael, as a student attending Florida Atlantic University, had met Chuck while the two of them were taking a martial arts class in Cuong Nhu—the same class where he also had met his Laura. The fact that Michael maintained good relationships with many of the people for whom he worked---long after he set off on his own entrepreneurial path---is a testament to how well regarded he was and what a good job he did while working for others. Of course he reached the ultimate in success when he became the "boss" of his own computer oriented business. He had what is called a great work ethic----he took on jobs in order to successfully complete them—even if that meant trying to do things differently than how others thought they should be done. He used some fabulous "people skills" to get through some very tough times in his work—with the final goal always being to successfully complete the job. Being an extraordinary problem solver certainly helped him get to the end of most jobs---the results always positive. He really did work many miracles during his working career, and there are those in the business world who would still sing his praises!

46

As we sat at a booth in the Palm Springs McDonalds restaurant one day when Michael was around three or four, Michael, as usual, was more interested in his toy then in the food that had accompanied the toy!! As he sat and played quietly, I took the time to feed Shara, noticing--out of the periphery of my vision--a young man sitting next to us who was totally intent on watching everything Michael was doing with his toy. The young man turned with a broad smile to his own mom and loudly let her know how tickled he was with what he saw Michael doing. He pointed and jabbered excitedly for long moments, and I became aware of the fact that those people who had been seated near us were beginning to get up and move away to other tables. Though others seemed annoyed with the young man's behavior, his obvious excitement for the toy and my little boy didn't bother me one bit. This young man was still his mom's little boy; Down's syndrome had given him the ability to always be able to show his delight in playing with toys and other children. When Michael realized he had an "audience," he looked to me as he picked up Shara's unused toy and pointed toward the young man! I knew he wanted to go play and share his toys so I said, "If it's okay with his mom." Of course it was more than okay with her. Michael introduced himself as he handed the young man one of the toys he held in his little hands, and they began to play with the toys on the table where the young man sat. It didn't seem to bother Michael that the young man did not talk to him or answer his questions—Michael just kept up the one-way conversation as only a three or four year old could!

Eventually, Michael drifted back to our table and actually began to eat his now cold hamburger and fries. As I was putting away Shara's things, I heard a soft voice, looked up, and saw the young man and his mom standing by our table: "Thank you so much," she said, "for letting your son play with mine. It means the world to me that someone cared enough about my boy not to let fear stop a wonderful moment---2 boys playing." When I looked at her more closely, I saw tears in her eyes, and I could not respond to her comment. I smiled but was at a loss for words.

Michael and I learned a very valuable lesson that day----we would certainly miss out on some very important experiences and people in our lives if we turned our backs in fear-- more pointedly if we allowed a fear of the unknown to determine our choices in life. Michael's instincts were "spot on" that day; even at the age of 3 or 4, he worked miracles!

From 2003 until 2006, when I had become the webmaster for our Laws of Life website, I enjoyed one of the best working situations with Michael that he and I ever had in our adult lives. Since I knew next to nothing about how to create a website, I eventually turned to Michael---with consent from the Board ---for his expertise and help in putting a website together for this non-profit group. I had been a teacher-participant---then a board member for this essay contest, which was held yearly and was open to all high school students---both in private schools and in public schools---in Palm Beach County. Laws of Life came about when representatives from the Templeton Foundation came to Palm Beach Gardens High to see if my Department Head, Rhonda Wilson, and I might be interested in getting involved in starting this essay contest for high school students in our county. Because their vision allowed for **all** students to become potential winners in the contest—we were able to see how successful a contest idea this was by looking at the first one they sponsored which began in Tennessee. Both Rhonda and I thought it would be a great opportunity, and our students would be able to benefit in a number of ways from a contest of this type. We saw the idea of the essay contest as a way to encourage students to identify something they were doing right in their lives and to write about it in such a way that others might benefit from their experiences. Sir John Templeton's idea, we felt, was to catch high school students doing good things in their lives and get them to share this with others. Our LOL Contest ran for approximately nine years, and our awards banquet featured some very inspiring and interesting people who came to honor our students and their efforts in writing. The novelist, James Patterson, was one of our most memorable speakers.

After a few years of hosting this contest, the Board of Directors discussed the idea of putting all our information on-line. This would certainly make it easier on those who had to generate and disperse all materials for the contest. It would also allow us to feature the students and their essays, and it offered a tangible and explanatory place for all teachers to use in order to encourage their own students to become involved in the contest. As webmaster, I turned to Michael for his expertise after I tried working with the son of a fellow board member who was a very intelligent high school student. The young man's idea for our website was highly technical and "glitzy" and would have been very expensive to create. Board members agreed with me that our website was meant to just be an informational and showcase site. Michael's beautiful design—simple and easy to navigate—turned out to be perfect---it was exactly what the board had wanted. He would listen to what my expectations were; then he would make them happen. Michael kept our site up and running for a very nominal fee of $9.00 a year! His wonderful blends of yellows and greens dominated the site. A palm tree he had planted in his own backyard became the model for our palm tree emblem. I think our website was light years ahead of the Georgia State site---the Georgia site contest spanned the entire state of Georgia while ours was just for one county in our state. Our site was much more inviting with its brilliant colors, its easily understood and insightful information, and its clever connecting bars that allowed users to easily surf from one page to the next. This was all due to Michael's input and talents. Secretly---working one-on-one with him---was a dream-come-true. It allowed me to have a type of relationship with him that few parents have the opportunity to enjoy---especially once children are grown and on their own!!

I remember when the idea of using computers at my job at Palm Beach Gardens High began in earnest---sometime in the 1990's. The English Department was given one computer, and we were each told to start learning the ins and outs of emailing. I didn't know anything about emailing and knew very little about using a computer; obviously I was not eager to get in line to use the department computer during my planning period! Besides, I had too much paperwork to do, keeping my plan book and grading students' papers. Eventually, we were all told that computers would play a huge part in our futures as classroom teachers, and we needed to learn all about how to use them. A fellow teacher, Scott Blake, and his department head, Linda Duhy, who were both "cracker-jack" business teachers began offering classes about computer use after school; these classes were directed toward those teachers who were interested in learning how to use the inevitable technology and for all who were interested in expanding their knowledge about using computers and how these skills could be transferred into the classroom experience.

With some degree of trepidation, I spoke with Michael and told him what was happening. His reaction was immediate and exuberant: "This is a fantastic idea! You will see that the computer can really assist you in your work---maybe even save you time---and certainly make many things easier for you and all teachers!" He assured me that he would help me all that he could---that I would probably surpass him by learning things that would be new even to him! Somehow, I doubted that last caveat!

Whenever I conquered something new on the computer, Michael was there playing the part of my most enthusiastic cheerleader, encouraging me to "keep up the good work!" And this role reversal wasn't lost on me. Michael's encouragement helped me to move much more easily into the technological millennium and to add a new and exciting dimension to my own private life---connecting me to the internet meant that I was now connected to a much bigger piece of the world.

I am so grateful for those fellow teachers whose patience and help knew no bounds---especially when they had to deal with students like me who felt way out of my element in computer classes. But I am most grateful to my loving son who never let my lack of knowledge or my shaky belief in myself get in the way of his being able to help me become adept at using a computer.

One of Michael's pleasures as an adult was connecting with all of his cousins and their families on his dad's side. (He always loved being with his cousins, Dorrie and Barbie, on my side of the family especially because we lived so close to them when we lived in the green house on Palm Road and he was just a little boy.) He looked forward to weddings and/or birthday celebrations because it gave him--and often his sister--the opportunity to interact with so many family members of his generation. And they certainly had fun when they all got together. There would be clowning around—this mostly performed by Michael---and some very serious "business-like" talk; but mainly, I think that they all enjoyed just being able to see each other and having fun. Michael once remarked to me that he wished we hadn't lost touch with his cousins on my side of the family, and I agreed. If I could have changed this situation, I certainly would have.

When Laura became a part of Michael's life---even before they were officially engaged----she was always included in all of the fun Michael shared with his cousins. How wonderful that his Aunt Gerry and Uncle Bennett had moved to south Florida because, eventually, all three cousins -first Cheryl then Erik then Joel- decided to settle here, too. How special it was that so many other family members---including cousins who live up north---would come down here to Florida for family celebrations. This provided a perfect opportunity for Michael to enjoy all their company----and he did just that!

50

Many young adults are not very interested in politics nor are they interested in getting involved in political movements; perhaps this is because they are just too busy getting their careers going. So I was really excited when I realized that Michael had become enmeshed in these activities. He began to share with me and with his dad---via e-mails---his active support for the philosophy of Ron Paul who was a doctor by trade and a well-known and well-liked Representative from Texas by choice. Ron Paul had decided to run for the office of the President of the United States in the 2008 election year. Much of what Ron Paul espoused as his beliefs as had to do with government and its responsibility to its people made perfect sense both to Michael and to Laura, and Michael was delighted to be able to inform us of all that he was learning. His enthusiasm and knowledge won us over, too! It was exciting to see him become involved in this campaign----giving of both his time and money---to help this particular candidate. We had many long and interesting phone chats and one-on-one talks about politics and the fate of our society and our personal responsibilities for these things. He made sure that he kept me and his dad "up" on all the important points that needed attention.

And since the birth of our precious Viktor in April of 2008, Michael seemed to be very concerned with the state of our educational system and all that was happening (or NOT happening) in that arena. In fact the last e-mail I was to receive from Michael----on Friday, May 22, 2009---was a link to read about some politician whose bizarre ideas about what needed to be done to "improve" educational systems were of very grave concern to Michael. He wanted my opinion about this person's ideas.

It is a very comforting feeling for any parent to know that the world in which we live is going to be a much better place for having our caring, activist adult children in it and to know that our adult children will accept the "torch" we pass on to them—a torch that will light their way to establish a better and an improved world for the next generation. This is what I think Michael was trying to do.

It's September, 2009 and it's been raining an awful lot lately---no complaints as we really need it----and I am reminded of the infamous flood of 1981---a flood that occurred after we had moved into our home in Trailwood----the house that Michael and Ed helped to build. When I say "flood," I am not exaggerating! Though, thankfully, our house was not under water, everything else was. There was no lake bank berm to be seen across the street as all the water just ran over and covered the road; and the water continued to flow into all the yards of the residents of Trailwood. The water was anywhere from one to two and a half feet deep! We looked out our windows only to discover that we had become an island unto ourselves as we were totally cut off from neighbors----surrounded by murky brown waters that were part lake water, and part rain water, and part canal water. The problem was that Trailwood had been developed like a saucer to the surrounding areas---all adjacent properties just drained into our development----the water sitting on their properties was seeking a place to settle and our lake became its main target for draining. When Ed drove home from work the day of the flood, he had to park his car out in front of our development---just off of Indiantown Road, and he had to wade in to get to our house. Fortunately, Michael and Shara and I were already home by the time the deluge began its worst damage. It was a bit scary to witness the devastation the sitting waters seemed to represent. We couldn't get into nor off of our property without having to wade a long way in water that surely contained dangerous inhabitants like poisonous snakes or even gators! Michael had gotten rid of a very large diamond back rattle snake—in our yard then on the berm across the street---shortly before the flood; and we had all been warned not to swim in the lake as someone had spotted a gator in the lake! Because of the flood (and my genuine fear of walking in the flood waters), Michael, Shara and I did not go to school the next school day, but after a day home and no change in the water level, Ed insisted he was going to brave the waters and go to work—he left wearing his boots and bathing suit and carrying his briefcase in one hand and his paper bag full of his change of clothes for work in the other!

After a few more days of being imprisoned in our home and waiting for the flood waters to recede, I realized that it was time for the kids and me to get back to school. Other neighbors had boats and canoes and were able to navigate our road to get out and go to work. But we did not have any boats. What we had were large inner tubes that had enclosed bottoms, and handles, and some paddles! These were "toys" the kids used in our swimming pool! Of course, Michael and Shara took advantage of these tubes and did quite a bit of exploring in the neighborhood. The whole time we were flooded, we also did not have any electrical power---certain foods could not be kept for long periods of time.

As it became most apparent---even after a TV news crew waded in to interview us---that the flooding problem was not going to go away anytime soon, I began trying to figure out what we were going to have to do---I had to get back to teaching and the kids needed to go to school---they actually hated missing so much school! They both even worried about having to miss so much school---they wanted to be there!   Of course the news media decided this flooding was a major news story; a young reporter named Chuck Weber---from Channel 12 (WPEC) I think---even braved the totally "yucky" water and waded to our house to interview us. Though daily shopping by Ed kept us fed, there were other problems that were more difficult to overcome---we needed electricity to run our water so flushing and bathing were next to impossible to accomplish. We decided that we would head on down to Grandpa and Nana Godwin's condo in Cresthaven so that we could get back to work, school and showers! Despite the fact that the condo had only two small bedrooms, my parents were more than willing to let us stay with them; but the big question was "how do we get out?" I was much too afraid to let the kids brave wading through that water. Besides, we had to take enough clothes with us and we could not leave our pet gerbil, Whiskers, to fend for himself! This would require that we make multiple trips in and out of our flooded home!

 Fortunately for us, the news interview that we had done generated the help we needed! Our neighbors wanted to be rescued and taken out of their homes as did our family; we were all eventually driven out of the neighborhood by very helpful guys who drove huge wheeled four-wheel drive vehicles that easily maneuvered through our flooded roads---we felt like we were riding in high sitting boats!! And in the Palm Beach Post Newspaper the day after our rescue, it was reported that our "family of **five** ---parents and **three** kids---had been rescued from our flooded neighborhood by this nice young man and his four-wheel drive!" Our rescuer had gotten the biggest kick out of Michael insisting that his pet, Whiskers, had to be rescued with us; and I had concurred by revealing the fact that Whiskers---inside his rather large terrarium--was, indeed, one of our close family members! The rescuers were there to get people out of their homes----not to rescue pets; but the young man allowed Whiskers and his cage to come out with us that day----and it's a good thing he did because Michael would never have consented to leave his pet behind! And so I now had three kids---not two!

Eventually, the flood waters receded, and we were able to get back into our development the usual way---by driving in our Toyota station wagon. And later, after an HOA meeting to discuss our problems with flooding and how to prevent future floods, we figured out a way to keep others' water from coming into and flooding Trailwood; we built a berm on the back lot lines all around the perimeter of Trailwood. And so we never flooded like that again!

52

From the time Michael was little and swimming in swim meets until he was a teen swimming in high school competition, the one activity his family participated in regularly was cheering him on to victory! I confess that I was the loudest---sometimes even straining my voice until I could no longer talk! And laryngitis is surely a detriment to a high school teacher who needed her voice to teach!! But even knowing that this might be the consequence of my loud cheering, once Michael was in that water, I had to be up and screaming him on to the successful finish. It wasn't until very late in Michael's swimming competition career that I learned of his secret----one that tickled him to no end. He revealed to me that when he was swimming, he could not hear anything other than a muffled roar each time he broke the surface to pull air into his lungs! What he heard was almost like a loud swoosh of air, and he never really was aware of it most of the time he swam!

So, I wondered, what was he thinking when he was in the water swimming competitively? He told me once that he liked to work out difficult math problems when he swam! He also liked to work out very complete plans for his up-coming weekend; but perhaps the more immediate thoughts he had while swimming had to do with what he wanted to eat when the competition was done! Did I waste my voice cheering for him those many times he swam? I don't think so because he knew we were all there, his whole family, for him----wanting him to achieve whatever he wanted to achieve.

As a family with the summer relatively "free", we spent many days and nights playing in our pool in the backyard of our Trailwood home. Ed and I often joked that while other families went on expensive and/or long family vacations in the summer months, we spent our vacations in our fabulous pool!! It was, as I've already said, a good-sized pool----20' by 40'—a perfect rectangle, and it was only 6' deep at the deepest end of the pool. Michael and Shara and I simply loved to spend our summer time in that pool. Marco Polo was one of the preferred games we played; and so was diving to the bottom of the pool in an effort to retrieve items that had been tossed there for that competitive purpose. We all liked to race each other to accomplish obtaining the items first, and when we formed teams to do this, everybody playing wanted to be on Michael's team because he was the fastest swimmer and the one who invariably would retrieve the items before anyone else could! We had rafts and inner tubes to float on top of the water's surface; and we had beach balls that we tossed around like "hot potatoes!" Our pool always had the same wonderful smell about it. (I could be brought, in a round-about way, blindfolded to the pool and always recognize our own pool's unique smell!) Our pool never was troubled with a chlorine smell like so many pools were. Its smell was just a clean, clear, pleasant and inviting smell. Definitely, the expert way in which both Ed and Michael meticulously took care of the pool resulted in this inviting smell and clear sparkling water that was reflected in our pool.

Every year that we lived at the Trailwood house, we couldn't wait until the pool was warm enough for us to jump in and begin our pool-fun-antics----and it always seemed to be "warm enough"---by the kids' standards---long before we adults were ready to brave gingerly putting our toes in without freezing those digits off!! The miracle that is youth...

For years when we lived in the Trailwood house, we did not use the air-conditioning. We simply kept the windows opened wide and the ceiling fans whirring on high all throughout the hot, sultry summer months. During those summers when we were on vacation from school, we dressed in bathing suits, and there were few times we were uncomfortable because of the heat. Ed and I thought that besides saving money, we were also doing things "right"-----our kids were not being "spoiled" by fake air---they were breathing nature's own sweet air! Wasn't fresh air supposed to be better for asthmatics and for those who suffered with allergies? We even drove around in our car with all the windows down----sans air-conditioning----and sang our way to wherever it was we were headed. Who knows if this practice of not having the air on in our home or car was good or not for Michael's health? The few times we did turn on the air-conditioning, we did not notice any difference in Michael's health issues!

We continued to enjoy the fresh and natural air until one day in 1990. On a sunny June day, I decided that life was just too short---and if this was true, we should go ahead and live it in total comfort! I turned on the air-conditioning for good that day, and we quickly adapted to being in a closed-up, air-conditioned home. And from time to time we would ask each other, "How did we EVER live through the summers without air-conditioning?" We couldn't believe that we had survived the awful heat all those years!!

(This is meant to be a clarifying aside: the white 1968 Camaro, which had been my very first car purchased without any monetary assistance from any family members---and which had been purchased after I obtained my first teaching position at Riviera Beach High School----was still one of our family cars when the kids were growing up. It is significant to note that this car NEVER had air-conditioning nor anything else considered an "extra." It was a bare-bones car that offered only heat to its owners! So, we were not practicing our altruism when it came to riding in this car---it was pre-determined by circumstance!)

55

Michael was always the "go to" guy. If there was a problem that needed to be solved or something that needed to be fixed or even something that needed to be figured out, Michael was the logical choice of whom to turn to for the help in figuring everything out---successfully. This was the case even when he was a little boy! And he seemed to thrive on being able to help figure out these problems! In his adulthood, this scenario was a constant. Technologically, he was heads above everyone else, always finding the right answer to a problem. At home, he could fix things that others had given up on, making those things work again or for longer than anyone could have hoped. We had a sit-down lawn mower when we lived at our Trailwood home---a lawn mower on which we should have painted a big picture of a lemon!! It rarely worked properly when I needed to mow our yard. But Michael would "fiddle" and "tinker" with its laboring parts until he got that mower moving again---long after Ed and I had given up hope that it would be able to mow again!

Michael had such an imagination. He could create whatever it was that was needed simply by thinking up a solution then working on the problem systematically---and his workmanship was always at a professional level! It was hard to believe that a person so young could produce such superior work! Every year he would come to work with me and help me decorate my classroom. He knew I liked to have things put up all around my classroom that were both colorful and useful. All this work was completed in just a few days during the pre-school period before a new school year began. Michael was always the very best "go to" guy in the world, and many people who came into his life over the years were delighted to discover this attribute in him. It contributed to a big part of the miracle that was Michael.

I think if I had to pick Michael's favorite eating holiday, that holiday would most likely be Thanksgiving. (The Seder would run a close second!) I've already mentioned that Halloween was probably his favorite holiday! Anyway, I remember when he and Laura were in the beginning days of their "couple-hood"; they used to plan to be at our home for the Thanksgiving dinner; then they would rush up to Laura's parents' place to eat with her family! It was truly a full day for them---in more ways than one!

When Michael finally asked for Laura's hand in marriage, placing a ring on her finger, he began to learn that compromise was an art he had to employ so that he could successfully juggle all of the necessary changes that he was going to have to make in his life! As Thanksgiving approached that year, Michael and I were speaking on the phone, and he mentioned how difficult it was to decide what to do on that day. Laura's family enjoyed celebrating this holiday, loving to bring together family and friends for a wonderful day of feasting and laughing! On the other hand, he really enjoyed all the traditional foods we served at our Thanksgiving table and the games we had fun playing after we stuffed ourselves! The question, he lamented, was "How can we be at both places or worse—how can we be separated from each other while we go alone to our family's Thanksgiving?" The answer was mine to give. I told him that I thought he needed to go with Laura to her family's celebration---that was the right thing to do. I couldn't explain why I felt this was the right thing to do----it just was. Michael lamented aloud the loss of not sharing all that he looked forward to---the things we ate, the games we played, and the "goofing off" that was always a part of this holiday!

Fortunately for all of us, after Michael and Laura got married, we all decided that we should celebrate Thanksgiving together---usually at the Powell's home on North Hutchinson Island in Martin County. One time we celebrated the holiday meal at our home, and several of the last years, we enjoyed eating and laughing in Laura and Michael's home!

When Michael was a boy---and we were living at Trailwood----we even had fun guests sitting at our table for the Thanksgiving meal---a meal usually served in the late afternoon—around 3:30 or so. One year Uncle Bennett and Michael's cousin Cheryl came---the rest of their family --- Aunt Gerry, Erik, and Joel—were still up in Massachusetts. One time we were fortunate enough to have Shara's diving coaches, Michele and Jose Rocha and their two wonderful dogs, Nico and Mico, come for Thanksgiving dinner. Yes, I fixed "plates" for the dogs!! (Michele's maiden name was "Mitchell"---she was a two time silver medalist in the 1984 Los Angeles and the 1988 South Korean Summer Olympics. One of her fellow divers for the men's team was the famous gold medalist, Greg Louganis. Michele's 10m platform event also won her a gold medal at the 1987 Pan American Games. Jose was a nationally known diver from Mexico who represented his country in the 1984 summer Olympics, and he was also an NCAA Champion diver who won many awards as a member of the Auburn University swim/dive team.)   Michele and Jose were wonderful people and so much fun to have at our table on one of our favorite holidays of the year! Michele brought one of her family's traditional foods for the holiday---a Jell-O salad that was very popular at our table that day!!

Of course Nana and Grandpa Godwin always spent the holiday with us---Nana made Michael's favorite pumpkin pie----and, well, we ALL enjoyed her pumpkin pie! While I was never able to re-create Nana's famous pumpkin pie, I have been able to do a good job of re-creating her yummy apple pie---not one of Michael's favorite pies. So, every year I would have to order at least two ten inch pumpkin pies from our Publix store's bakery.---one pie for Michael to take home and have all to himself and the other for the rest of us to share after our Thanksgiving meal. I tried so many times to make a pumpkin pie---any pumpkin pie---but I just can't make it happen!! I can make a wonderful pumpkin pudding-like dish, but it's just NOT the same! Of course Uncle Bob and his family would come for the holiday meal, too. We were even lucky enough to have Grandpa and Grandma Green (Bob's first wife's family) come to our home for Thanksgiving dinner a couple of times, too. I guess you could say that this holiday really was a way for us to say "thanks" to all of the many people we have met in our lives and befriended and to all those whom we have loved all our lives as family.

I have alluded to the "look" of serene joy that would come over Michael's face when he was doing something very special---it was a look of pure peace and ecstasy---a look that said "paradise is like this." When Michael was 2 and rode the horse at Judy's house---the one that was 17 hands tall---he wore that look; when, at the age of 4 or 5, he took a pony ride at the circle just outside the entrance to Dreher Park Zoo in West Palm Beach, his face shone with that look—even though his little sister was crying and sobbing to be removed from her own pony; when Michael first realized that Whiskers was really going to be able to come home with us, Michael's face reflected that he was in his personal zone of paradise; when he received then later set up and had running his TRS80, he just sat and stared at it as if seeing something none of the rest of us would ever be able to see; and when he went to Disney World and met the characters for the first time, he was wearing his mile-wide smile and he had that look again---a look of sheer bliss! He enjoyed hugging Mickey and Minnie Mouse, slapping hands (feathers?) with Donald Duck and goofing off with Goofy, but I think he had the most fun with Pluto.

When Michael was around 6 years old and Shara was 4, we decided that if we wanted the kids to be able to see most of the Disney characters, we needed to make reservations for Breakfast with the Characters, which at that time was being held on the Princess Lily---a docked paddlewheel boat on Lake Buena Vista. Ed and I thoroughly enjoyed watching our two kids giggle and play with all the characters. Michael would stop and just stare in awe as each character bounded into the room in which we were seated for breakfast. The characters worked their way over, finally, to our table---and the giggling and laughing would grow into a cacophony of sound. Aunt Janie and Jackie and her cousin Randy were all sitting at the table with us---what fun it was to see and hear all these kids happy and thoroughly engaged in pure, nonsensical fun!

Another time we visited Disney World, we took Michael and Shara to the Character Meal at the Contemporary Hotel, and we were feted and entertained by the famous Chipmunks, Chip and Dale. Perhaps that look on Michael's face was just a way for his deep-seated happiness to escape and shine through----but I think it was so much more---it was an extreme form of inner happiness that few of us would ever be able to experience in our lives. I'm glad I was able to see this on the face of our precious Michael!

I remember a funny "guy" who came to live with us when Michael was not quite 2 years old. His name was "Goofy Gus." In fact Michael not only helped to name him----he also helped to make him! I had wanted Michael to have one of the "new" dolls that helped to teach children how to tie laces, button buttons in buttonholes, how to zip and unzip a zipper, how to close snaps, and how to use Velcro closures. (Michael was most fascinated with sandspurs at the time and how they stuck to his pants---and who knows? If he had been older and in the right place at the right time, he might have been the one to discover and be the developer of Velcro!) That store-bought teaching doll was, I admit, a very expensive item to place on the wish list that Nana and Grandpa Godwin had requested I make for them. When my dad saw that I was asking for a DOLL for his only grandson, he emphatically said, "Absolutely NOT!!! No grandson of mine is going to be playing with dolls!" I tried to explain to Michael's grandpa that the educational value of such a doll would have a positive impact on Michael's learning process; but my dad wasn't having any of this! And I came to accept the idea that my dad had come from a different and older generation----one that had a very hard time believing and accepting the fact that it was really "okay" for boys to have and show feelings for dolls. Many in my dad's generation considered it too "girlish" for boys to be playing with dolls---no matter what the educational value. (Just a year or so later, we had our Shara living with us, and there were numerous dolls to be found in her room. Interestingly enough, Shara wasn't much interested in playing with dolls; but by this time, Michael was taking care of his own "Joey" doll!! I really think that his youthful interest in dolls is why, as an older teen and adult, he bonded so well with children. His nephews, Tyler and Trevor, absolutely loved him and easily played with him at the beach on Folly Island, even though he was almost a stranger to them. They live in South Carolina; visits were few and far apart. Michael was like the Pied Piper of his neighborhood where he, Laura, and, finally, Viktor lived---when he was out on his gas-powered skateboard, the kids in the neighborhood would follow him, waiting for the turn they knew he was going to offer them!)

At the time I had placed the teaching doll on that list for my parents, my little family was, by necessity, on a very tight budget; we simply could not afford to purchase such an expensive luxury item. But not to be undaunted, Michael and I set out to make our own educational doll, using things we already had at home. I will admit I was not then nor am I now, the consummate "sewer" that my family members were and that many of my friends were (and still are!) I forged ahead with little talent and skill, but with a whole lot of love for and help from Michael. I made up a pattern of sorts out of an old white sheet, and Gus began to take shape. After staring at the cut-out sheet, Michael referred to it as "Gus." I don't remember why or where he got the idea for this name, but Gus it was. As Gus began to be more recognizable as a real doll, I took to calling him "Goofy" because what I was creating was certainly goofy-looking!!

For one thing, Gus was bigger than Michael---both taller and wider!! (Note to other non-sewers: it is much easier to make something big with your sewing machine than it is to try to sew something miniscule like doll-sized!) Gus sported yellow yarn hair, sparsely sewn at the top of his head—we used all the yarn we had on hand. His clothes were a mixed-match--made from material scraps we found at the bottom of my meager sewing bag! The buttons we ultimately used were fairly large red ones---I discovered that large button holes were easier to perfect than the smaller, normal-sized ones were. Besides, buttonholes get bigger as one "practices" sewing them, making large buttons a necessity! Gus's eyes were colored on by Michael----blue was his favorite color at the time, so blue the eyes became. (Later, we found a couple of blue buttons in Nana's button box and sewed them on Gus's proud face!) Michael and I found a partially used piece of red felt in my material bag, and we fashioned a rather large, broadly smiling mouth from this scrap; then we glued it on at a jaunty angle—this last totally Michael's idea! When anyone first met Gus, it was Gus's huge grin that they first responded to----stifling giggles! The zipper in Gus's blue pants was sewn in by hand after numerous attempts to sew it in by machine; and that zipper worked just fine after Michael and I applied an ample amount of hard soap up and down its "teeth." The zipper was a used one that I had rescued from a pair of Ed's old pants and probably hadn't been zipped or unzipped in years!! We used red shoe laces from a pair of Michael's old tennis shoes----he found them in his toy box---the toy box Ed and I had made for him that was clearly marked "My Stuff"—that's where Michael kept most of his "treasures." As he handed me the shoes with the dangling laces, I worried over the fact that there was no way I could make "shoes" for Gus. His feet were big, but they were also weirdly shaped---kind of flat and pointing sideways! But I shouldn't have worried because Michael had already addressed this dilemma. He handed me a pair of his old, whitish socks which fit Gus's miss-matched feet just fine. Michael set out then to color the socks to look like shoes with his brown permanent marker. I got busy cutting the holes in which we would be able to weave the laces. The snap we sewed onto Gus's outfit was truly the easiest part of this project. Under Gus's blue jacket (no, the jacket did not match the pants!), he wore an old t-shirt that had been Michael's. Michael picked this t-shirt out of the give-away bag, and we cut a long "V" into and down the back of the neckline; then I sewed the snap parts on either side of the flap the "V" created. Michael and I were done making Gus.

For a very long time, Michael did not want to be parted from Gus. He quickly learned to work all the "educational" tasks that Gus offered, and Michael learned all of these tasks on his own. But he continued to drag and/or carry Gus all over the place; and that heavy sheet-filled doll---who I already said was bigger and heavier than Michael ---bore an eerily strong resemblance to the scary looking clowns one finds in the scariest of horror movies!! Gus was certainly not ordinary looking by anyone's standards. Ed claimed that Gus's ears were inspired by his own----but that was not true because Gus's ears were much bigger than Ed's, and they stuck straight out from the side of his flattish head!

Most days, I would find Michael sitting or standing with or lying on Gus---I'd see them sitting in front of his toy box in his room, playing with toys; or they would be lying in front of the TV set in the family room, Michael practically on top of Gus, both intently watching Sesame Street; or they would be standing together at the front living room window, Michael's arm around Gus and holding him up while they leaned on the low window sill and just stared out at the neighborhood and its panorama of activities. Viktor's relationship with his Big Blue Bear and the interaction Viktor has with his bear remind me of Michael's attachment and interaction with his own Goofy Gus. Of course the BBB doesn't offer the option to learn how to lace, snap, button, and zip that Gus offered----but the hugging and/or sleeping with options are the same. Michael certainly loved his Gus just as Viktor loves his Big Blue Bear!

On a sunny day in August of 2000, I found myself sitting in the bleachers of the large and noisy Florida Atlantic University auditorium---surrounded by my family—Ed, Shara and Michael's Laura----watching the many black-robed students file into their folding chairs that were all set up on the floor of the auditorium; we were waiting for that one, most important computer science student who was about to reach his goal---a BS degree in Computer Science. At age 27, Michael had finally completed his studies and would be able to enter the work force with the papers that proclaimed him to be a certified expert in his field! Of course those of us who knew Michael, knew that he was a self-taught computer expert long before August 16, 2000. But as I sat there, thrilled to be a witness to his collegial success, I couldn't help remembering all that it took to get Michael to this day.

Once Michael graduated from high school, he had to face the reality that there was just not enough money saved for him to attend a very expensive but well-thought-of exclusive art college in Georgia. He was out of our home and living on his own and was supporting himself with a few good jobs when he decided that he wanted to attend Florida Atlantic University and get his degree in the computer field. I was delighted that he wanted to go to college---- especially since I had gotten my BA degree from the very same college! Ed and I gave him all the assistance that we could---both by helping him monetarily and by giving him all the moral support we could. It was not an easy road for Michael---he was older and had many personal responsibilities to juggle along with a full and vigorous college schedule. Michael literally fought to get his degree. He worked a full-time job while taking classes, and he paid for all of his living expenses. Fortunately, he did receive some help from student loans and grants. There were times when his ultimate goal seemed to be totally out of reach to him---times when he wanted to give up because it would be easier to just "work the ONE job." But he didn't quit—he persevered---and he pulled himself up by the boot straps and continued to take and pass the courses which put him on the path to obtain his degree. Even when he discovered that he had to take an extra semester because a Gordon Rule course that was required of him wasn't offered until the following semester, he did not let the frustration of having to wait yet another semester to graduate stop him from his ultimate goal. He was determined to get his Computer Science degree.

We all spotted him at about the same time in that sea of black robes and multi-colored tasseled mortarboards----his mile-wide-smile a beacon to us----as he jauntily walked to his seat. He wasn't looking for us in that huge crowd of proud family and friends; No, he knew that we were there with him, ready to celebrate this most special of days!!

60

Becoming Wednesday Nannies for Michael and Laura's Viktor was both rewarding and a source of great humor for Ed and me. Michael worked from home developing his computer systems design and programming/web design and support business. He soon discovered what Ed and I had secretly known from the moment Viktor joined their household---it was next to impossible to be a full-time dad to an infant all day **and** to get the work done that was necessary in order to sustain his burgeoning business!! Michael and Laura resolved this problem by interviewing and hiring a part-time nanny who would be responsible for Viktor and take care of all his needs while Michael was free to carry on with his daily work. (At the same time, Laura would be able to continue her work for Palm Beach County in its Engineering Department.)

Ed and I had offered our services to the new parents, but they—wisely---chose not to accept our offer, knowing that four days a week with an infant would be very tiring, indeed---as it was even for young adults!!! So, we settled on a plan that would have us become Viktor's nannies on Wednesday of each week. We were thrilled to be able to do this as it provided us with the opportunity to spend time with not just our newest grandson, but with Michael and Laura, too!

From the beginning of our most important "assignment," we were given explicit directions about what Michael and Laura expected us to accomplish each Wednesday that we spent with Viktor. Besides the usual duties of a nanny such as feeding, changing, rocking, and walking with and talking to Viktor, there were more, shall we say in-depth, educational issues that needed to be explored. There were books to be read to the baby; there were laminated posters depicting all sorts of valuable facts---from the seemingly simple ABC's to the very challenging Periodic Table---that had to be carefully introduced into the daily curriculum. There was also a colorful map of the United States and one of the World that had to be cleverly used in the instruction process. We were also to include flashcards that were deemed "age-appropriate" for Viktor. These flashcards were (and continue to be) a great favorite of Viktor's-----he especially liked to chew on them and continues his pleasure in bending them!! But he has learned all of them!

Along with the more cerebral tasks of Viktor's educational process, we nannies were also expected to address his physical growth needs. One Wednesday, we were summoned, while Viktor napped, by Michael and asked to join him in the family room. He invited us to have a seat so that we could talk about what Michael and Laura perceived was Viktor's "alarming" inability to crawl correctly. Ed and I looked at each other with questioning eyes, then Michael went on to explain to us that Viktor's dragging motion (one in which he crawls like a ground soldier) was going to interfere with Viktor's ability to learn---it was literally stunting his intellectual growth!! Ed and I looked at each other again then quickly looked away. Michael went on to explain what would be necessary for us to do in order to get Viktor where he needed to be: Michael's plan was going to get Viktor on the right crawling track!! In demonstration, Michael dropped to the floor and showed us the proper crawling technique that was expected from babies in Viktor's age bracket. He carefully explained each step for us and wanted us to begin this phase of Viktor's education just as soon as the baby awoke from his nap.

Being the good, accommodating, and smart grandparents that we were (and certainly being cognizant of the fact that we did not want to jeopardize or lose our precious nanny jobs), we plucked Viktor from his crib when he woke up, changed his diaper, fed him, then placed him on the family room floor prepared to give him his first "crawl-right" lesson. But I just could not do it without cracking up; Ed, however, was a Crawling Teacher Champ. He crawled all over the floor, demonstrating for Viktor, the proper knee and leg movements over and over again; he then encouraged the baby to try it by moving Viktor's legs and knees in the appropriate crawl positions. Ed must have worked with Viktor a good 10 minutes when it became apparent that Viktor was tiring of all this physical exertion. So, we all just sat on the floor and played with Viktor's toys and tickled him and kissed him each time he climbed into our laps.

Later that same evening, after we returned home from our joyous nanny job, we received an excited phone call from Michael. He was calling to report that Viktor was now crawling in the intellectually appropriate way!! Ed and I took our "Best teachers" and Magical teachers" sobriquets given to us by an appreciative Michael in stride---and stifling giggles behind our hands!! We knew that Viktor was just ready to crawl---most probably because he wanted to escape the tortuous, silly lessons he'd had to endure on how to crawl correctly!

Speculation

When someone is suffering from multiple, mental and/or health issues, loving them with your whole heart and soul is sometimes just not enough.

It is apparent to Ed and me now that Michael must have been suffering from depression probably from the time when he was 16 and feeling "different" and tried to self-medicate by experimenting with certain drugs. We thought at 16 he was just suffering some form of teenage angst---just trying to assert himself as an independent son from his protective parents. As a high school teacher---one who really cared about and got involved with her students---I was embarrassed to discover that my own son had gotten involved with drugs. I couldn't believe it—felt that it was a personal slap in my face because we had spent so much time talking openly about drugs and the dangers drugs imposed on the people who chose to use them. My beautiful, gifted, Eagle Scout son had involved himself in the evil world of drugs---had tried to take the miracle away from his dad and I. I felt like a failure as a mom----even his little sister knew he was experimenting with drugs----too afraid of losing the tenuous hold on her relationship with her beloved older brother to risk telling us what was going on with him. But to reveal her awful knowledge to us was NOT her job! For long periods of time, I felt like I should have known—should have suspected what Michael was doing---and I should have stopped it. But I realized eventually that this was not something I could have known. He was very clever--- so much cleverer than I ever was! I now believe that Michael was trying to escape ---maybe from an awful, dark pain which would pursue him throughout his life--- and he did those drugs at 16/17 in order to find some peace. When he attempted suicide, the doctor assured us that this was not really a serious attempt on Michael's part to take his own life. The cuts on his wrist were not deep—they were superficial; but we had Michael Baker Acted just the same. (To Baker Act someone is a means of providing individuals with emergency services and temporary detention for mental health evaluation and treatment when required, either on a voluntary or an involuntary basis.)

Unfortunately, Michael was too smart for his own good when it came to his month long stay at a facility for young and troubled teenagers. He arrived in this second facility after being removed from the first one he had been whisked off to---this first place was a very expensive, country-club like resort for troubled teens where we saw in their glossy brochure that they employed chefs who wore real chef hats as they served the teenagers their lobster!! No lie!! When Michael got to the second facility, he was able to control most of the staff---including the doctors---as he easily manipulated them to see things his way. I think his anger and his high degree of intelligence may have kept him from getting the help he needed. He expressed his idea--- in not so many words---that he thought that we just wanted to be rid of him---nothing could be further from the truth! And we made sure he heard this message often! Anyway, in typical Michael fashion, he had the doctors believing that I was the cause of all of the turmoil and problems going on in our home. He convinced them that because I was going through the "change," I was always acting irrationally and couldn't be reasoned with at all. (Remember---I had had a complete hysterectomy before I was married and would never experience the "change"----a fact that those doctors never discovered!) Of course I did contribute to all of the problems our family experienced, but I wasn't the reason Michael turned to drugs.

When Michael left us at age 17 in the spring of 1990, drugs may have been the problem but they were just a "band-aid" for the symptoms of his real problems. I wish I had known that at the time. When my parents were killed in June of the same year, I secretly harbored the hope that Michael would "come to his senses" and move back with us. But he never did. And though he did come out to the house when I called to give him the news about his beloved grandparents---who had been killed in an automobile accident while on their way to their yearly college classes in Virginia---he was less than friendly, obviously angry with us and the world, and he left shortly after he had come. We kept track of him as best we could, and we arranged and went to therapy sessions as a family. We would pick him up and take him to the therapist's office in Jupiter. Gary Wylin was an exceptional therapist who was not easily manipulated by our smart son. His insights helped us immensely throughout this unpleasant period of our family's past. We would also give Michael a ride back to the place where he was living. His anger with us (and himself I came to realize) didn't really dissipate until after his sister's 1993 high school graduation—which, to her extreme delight, he attended. She broke from the graduate line and ran to hug him as he stood smiling and waving to her!! He was the best graduation gift she could ever get!! He came back to the house to visit, and from then on, we **all** worked hard to reestablish and build our relationships with each other.

Until the fall of 2008, we did not suspect that anything was wrong. In fact Michael was the epitome of a successful 35 year old entrepreneur, a loving husband and daddy, a very successful businessman owning his own thriving computer consulting business, a young man who was, thankfully, closer to us than ever. Little did we know that he was "keeping a lid" just barely on his darkest secret---he was suffering from a depression so strong, so painful that it would become his terminal illness. It was in the fall of this same year that Michael began to confide in me just a little----telling me that he felt bad most of the time and was unhappy with his life---he complained about his diagnosis of tinnitus. (Tinnitus is the perception of sound within the human ear in the absence of corresponding external sound.) Though I, too, suffer from this same illness, I felt that Michael was experiencing a difficult time adjusting to and accepting the fact that there was no cure for this diagnosis. I also thought that he was suffering from depression. (I had suffered with this illness most of my adult life without receiving any help, and I knew of its devastating effects. In 2002 I had finally gotten relief from depression by being prescribed a medication that quickly restored my well-being.) Michael went to a psychiatrist who prescribed anti-depressant drugs and told him to find and go to see a therapist—then he sent him on his way. A very upset Michael told me much later about this first meeting with the psychiatrist: he said he broke down and cried in the man's office and after a few minutes, the guy led him out of his office and into the waiting room and advised Michael not to leave until he could pull himself together enough to drive home! Over the next few months, Michael claimed that he was feeling better and was more capable of dealing with his life and its inherent problems. Then around January of 2009, he had another "meltdown." He called and talked to me for hours. Ed stayed with me and helped me to talk and listen to our son. Michael talked about feeling like a failure, like he was trapped and that he had such guilt over feeling this way---because he couldn't control things. He said he felt angry much of the time. I suggested that the medication was not working correctly and that he needed to see a doctor again---and he needed to get an appointment with a therapist. Since he mentioned anger issues to me, I told him that the medication I had been prescribed had certainly taken care of most of my anger issues and maybe it might work for him. I had tried and given up after 4 attempts to find an appropriate medication for my problem and didn't want him to give up. I did remind him to tell his doctor that he was adopted because even if the medicine worked on me, there was no guarantee it would work on Michael's depression. Again, Michael went to the same doctor and got another anti-depressant drug prescribed---and after a short while, he said he was definitely feeling better. But Ed and I and Laura were still very concerned because he was not trying to find and set up an appointment with a therapist. He kept putting the idea off—explaining that he was feeling better—even though the tinnitus was driving him crazy. He and I discussed this annoying diagnosis, and I shared with him some of my own coping skills. Sometime in April, he called me again and revealed that he wasn't feeling well. I begged him to see another doctor. I had been working with Mary Hinton to get the names of good doctors who specialized in Michael's particular diagnosed illnesses. In late April one particular name was suggested, and he seemed to be the perfect fit for Michael because not only did he specialize in Michael's diagnosed illnesses, but he also worked exclusively with young adults in Michael's age bracket. But for 3 weeks Michael didn't call that doctor---and we would bring up the idea of calling the doctor as much as we dared---we did not want to risk angering him by seeming to push him too hard, and he seemed to be feeling better—even told his dad he was feeling really good.

Laura told us that when she stood at Michael's desk On Tuesday, May 26, 2009---the day after he had chosen to leave us forever--- that she had found a print-out of the email I had sent to him in early May with the names and addresses of the doctor and therapist. He had printed this information on Friday, May 22, 2009, and Laura said that he'd written "call next week." I like to believe that Michael was fighting his illnesses to the very end. He was going to try another doctor-- perhaps reluctantly because I think that he had lost hope that anyone could help him. One of our very special friends, Edna Runner, said it so well: "Michael was in a lot of pain and God said, 'Come on home.' And he did." I will always remember him as our brave, valiant, humorous, creative, bright and loving son. He was our miracle boy!

Dilemma

It has taken me a little over a year to write and type up this memoir of our son. It is now August, 2010—that's 1 year and 3 months since we lost our precious Michael. And, of course, our lives have been changed forever. Ed is still trying to come to grips with his deep grief, but there are signs that he is beginning to heal; Laura is doing extremely well with her job, being a successful single parent to our precious Viktor, and putting her life back on track one day at a time; Viktor is happily growing by leaps and bounds both physically and intellectually, and he continues to be a joy for all of us—a good "mix" of his daddy and his mom; Shara continues to be our strength despite the fact that she has so many obligations to fulfill within her own life—to her family and to her jobs—she loves us unconditionally; and I am also moving forward, making plans that are both short and long term in nature, and I am able to feel comfort from and to embrace with strength all my good memories of our lives with Michael---and I continue making wonderful memories with our friends and family, and particularly with Laura and Viktor.

If there is one sure lesson I have learned in my years of experience, it is that life, by its very definition, is never exactly what we expect it should be. There are twists and turns that change the course of our lives. Some of these twists and turns are good for us, but some are hard for us to endure. We stumble through as we navigate the unknown, the unexpected, and the unfathomable.

And oh how we are stumbling even still. Four weeks ago as our Laura sat with her attorney-- in conference over a contested insurance company's decision regarding our son's death-- the lawyer reiterated some information that included the statement that Michael was left-handed. It was said in passing, without any suggestion that this information was in any way important information. Laura heard the statement and reacted as all of us who knew Michael would: "But Michael wasn't left-handed." In all the months since Michael left us, we have struggled with the "whys" of what we had thought was his choice to leave us. Laura has never wavered in her belief that Michael would not have taken his own life in spite of the reports to the contrary. I kept asking the same question over and over: But why had Michael printed out the names of the new doctor and therapist just 2 days before he left us—names I had emailed to him in early May? Wasn't this deliberate act proof that he had decided to call and make an appointment—to try again to get help? And Ed would wonder aloud, "Why wasn't there a note for us left on his computer—at least for Laura and Viktor? He would have left a note to explain." And we all wondered why he had---within just a few days of leaving us---sought out and won over 2 new clients? We all witnessed his rejoicing in this business "coup."

And now we have a new, upsetting and disturbing—but very important question to ask: Why did everyone involved in the case just assume that Michael was left-handed? The deputy who was the lead investigator—the one who labeled Michael's death a suicide—never ascertained if Michael was left-handed. The woman who performed the autopsy also did not question which hand was Michael's dominant hand. Both of these experts wrote in their reports that the gun was in Michael's left hand and **only** his left-hand fingerprints were found on the weapon.

We who love him are left with the thought that perhaps Michael's last act here on earth was not one made by choice that day. Was he deeply depressed? Without a doubt. Was he upset that the prescribed medication was no longer working for him? Most assuredly. Did he remove the gun from the safe with dark thoughts running through his mind? Yes. But, did he—at the moment the weapon was fired—have the intent to take his life?

The gun was not in his right hand—his dominant hand. He was not ambidextrous. The answer to this last question is abundantly clear to me and to the family: Absolutely not!

Maybe this "newly-brought-to-light" piece of information will ease the pain those who love Michael have felt---maybe knowing this will help Viktor deal a little better with the loss of his daddy when it is time for him to have his questions answered. And just maybe this will serve as a positive warning to those of you who may find yourselves in similar circumstances----search for the whole truth. And to those who may wish to walk that dangerous and scary "edge": Do not let your choices be taken from you because of an "accident" or a "non-intended" act.

For those of you who are reading this and who have that same dark, painful secret: Please realize that you are **_so_** loved----by a spouse, sibling, child, parents, grandparents, aunts, uncles, cousins, and your friends, and we will ALL be forever changed if we lose you because you feel you can't reach out to any one of us.

PLEASE give us the opportunity to help you. Let us keep the miracle of you alive.

www.ingramcontent.com/pod-product-compliance
Lightning Source LLC
Chambersburg PA
CBHW040905020526
44114CB00037B/65